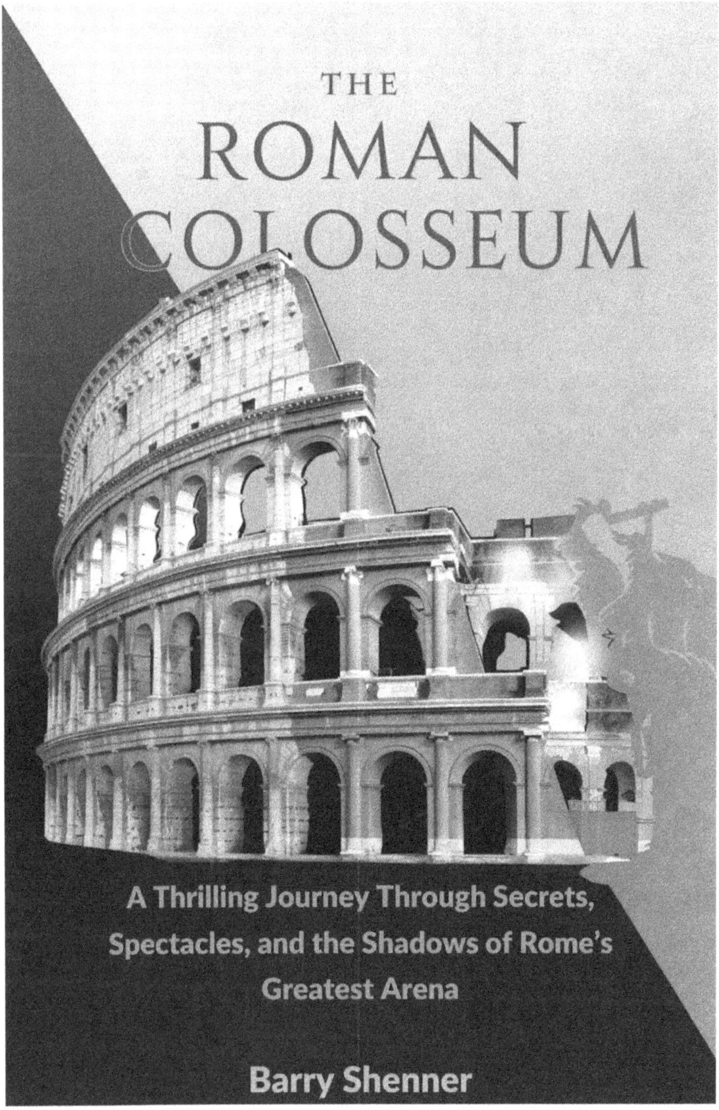

THE ROMAN COLOSSEUM

A Thrilling Journey Through Secrets, Spectacles, and the Shadows of Rome's Greatest Arena

Barry Shenner

The Roman Colosseum

A Thrilling Journey Through Secrets, Spectacles, and the Shadows of Rome's Greatest Arena

Barry Shenner

COPYRIGHT

Copyright © [2024] [Barry Shenner].

All rights reserved. No part of this book may be reproduced, stored in a retrieval system, or transmitted in any form or by any means, electronic, mechanical, photocopying, recording, or otherwise, without prior written permission of the author, except in the case of brief quotations used in critical reviews and articles.

Published by [**Barry Shenner**]

CONTENTS

INTRODUCTION 1
THE BIRTH OF A COLOSSUS 7
    Rome's Ambition: The Era of the Flavian Emperors 8
    Engineering Marvel: Building the Colosseum 13
    A Day in Ancient Rome: The Colosseum Unveiled 19
    The Anatomy of an Arena 24
SPECTACLE AND SOCIETY 29
    Entertaining the Masses: The Purpose of the Games 30
    Gladiators: Heroes, Slaves, and Legends 35
    Beasts in the Arena: Venationes and Beyond 42
    Sea Battles and Set Pieces: Beyond Gladiatorial Combat ... 47
BEHIND THE SCENES 53
    The Logistics of Spectacle 54
    The Economy of the Colosseum 60
    Voices from the Past: Spectators and Participants 66
    The Ethical Dilemma of Roman Entertainment 72
DECLINE AND TRANSFORMATION 79
    The Colosseum's Fall: Rome's Changing Landscape 80
    Medieval and Renaissance Colosseum 85
    Rediscovering the Colosseum: Archaeology and Restoration 90
    A Global Symbol: The Colosseum Today 96

THE COLOSSEUM IN CONTEXT **101**
    Comparisons with Other Roman Amphitheaters........... 102
    The Colosseum's Influence on Architecture.................. 108
    Myths, Legends, and Misconceptions........................... 114
    The Colosseum as a Metaphor..120
CONCLUSION..**125**
APPENDICES.. **131**
    Timeline of the Colosseum's History........................... 131
    Glossary of Terms and Key Figures.............................. 134

INTRODUCTION

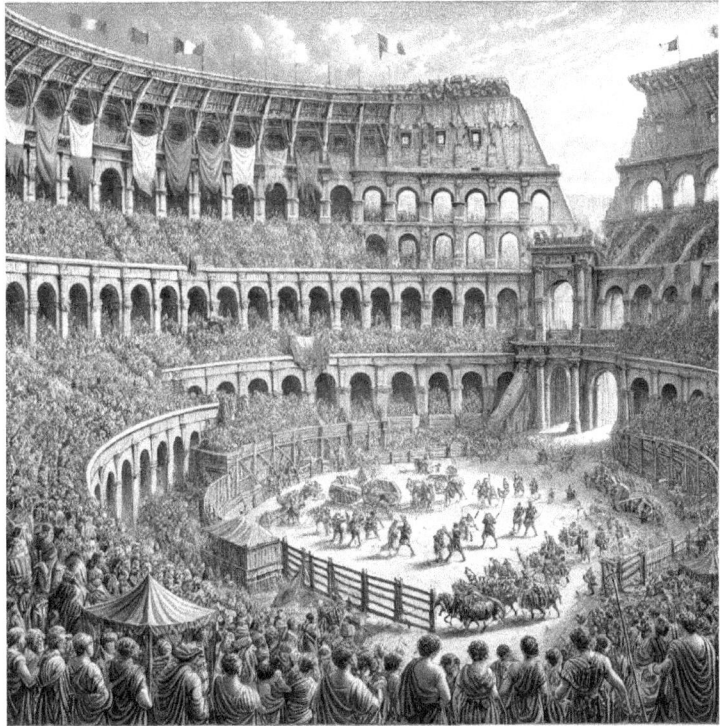

Why the Colosseum Endures: A Monument of Power and Spectacle

In the heart of modern Rome, amidst the hustle and bustle of traffic and the hum of tourists snapping selfies, stands a silent witness to the grandeur of an ancient civilization: the Colosseum. Even in its weathered state, the amphitheater exudes an aura of strength and permanence, a stark reminder of Rome's immense power and ambition. But what is it about this nearly 2,000-year-old structure that continues to capture the imagination of millions?

The Colosseum was not merely an arena; it was a stage for the greatest spectacles the world had ever seen. It was where gladiators fought for glory, where wild beasts roared in dramatic confrontations, and where emperors used elaborate shows to demonstrate their dominance and generosity. Built by the Flavian emperors, it symbolized the might of Rome, a gift to the people and a testament to their empire's engineering genius.

Yet, its enduring appeal lies not only in its history of spectacle but also in its contradictions. The Colosseum is both a symbol of human ingenuity and a haunting reminder of human cruelty. It represents the heights of architectural brilliance and the depths of a culture's appetite for violence. It is this duality that keeps the

Colosseum relevant, sparking debates about the ethics of entertainment and the complexity of human nature. To understand why the Colosseum endures is to explore these layers of its identity, peeling back the myths to reveal truths that resonate even today.

The Legacy of Rome's Great Arena: Then and Now

When the Colosseum's inaugural games commenced in 80 CE, it was a spectacle of unimaginable scale. Thousands gathered to witness the debut of an arena that could seat over 50,000 spectators. Gladiators clashed with one another in brutal contests, exotic animals from distant lands fought for survival, and naval battles were simulated in a flooded arena. It was a theater of extremes—a celebration of Roman ingenuity and a statement of imperial supremacy.

Over the centuries, however, the Colosseum's role evolved. With the fall of the Roman Empire, its purpose shifted from entertainment to practicality. It became a fortress, a quarry, and even a place of Christian worship. Despite earthquakes and neglect, the Colosseum survived, its stones whispering stories of a bygone era.

Today, the Colosseum is more than a historical relic; it is a global icon. It draws millions of visitors annually, serving as both a tourist destination and a symbol of Rome's rich heritage. The amphitheater's image adorns postcards, films, and textbooks, making it one of the most recognizable landmarks in the world. It has transcended its original purpose, becoming a metaphor for resilience, a touchstone for architectural innovation, and a lens through which we view the complexities of ancient Rome.

But its legacy is not without challenges. The Colosseum faces threats from pollution, climate change, and the wear and tear of countless feet treading its ancient stones. Efforts to preserve it are ongoing, a testament to its significance not only as a Roman artifact but as a piece of global history.

The Journey Through History Begins

To walk through the Colosseum's arches is to step into a time machine. Imagine the roar of 50,000 voices echoing through the air, the clash of metal, and the feral growls of beasts. Picture the vivid colors of the spectators' tunics, the smell of roasted meats from vendors, and the palpable tension as the emperor gives the signal for a gladiator's fate. It is a journey into the heart of a civilization that shaped much of the Western world.

This book invites you to embark on that journey. Together, we will uncover the stories of the people who built, inhabited, and ultimately abandoned this magnificent structure. We will explore the Colosseum's architecture and the innovation that made it possible. We will delve into the lives of the gladiators, the emperors, and the everyday Romans who made the games possible. And we will trace its transformation from a bustling center of entertainment to a silent monument of the past.

Along the way, you will encounter tales of courage and cruelty, of triumphs and tragedies, and of the eternal struggle between the human thirst for power and the desire for meaning. This is not just a history book; it is an exploration of what the Colosseum represents about us—our capacity for greatness and our propensity for excess.

THE BIRTH OF A COLOSSUS

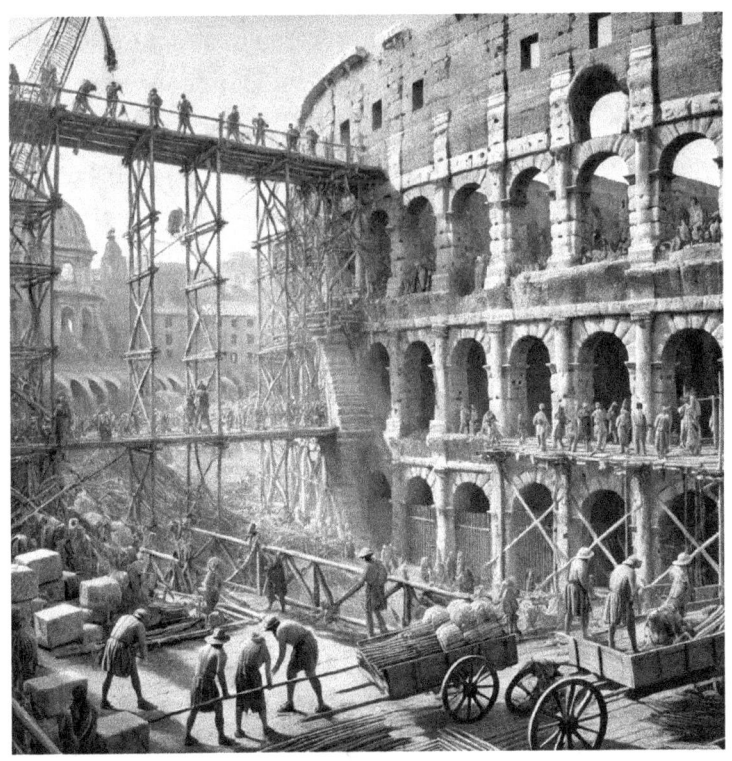

Chapter 1:

Rome's Ambition: The Era of the Flavian Emperors

The Colosseum—a name that evokes images of gladiators, roaring crowds, and the grandeur of ancient Rome. It is one of the most iconic structures in the world, a monument that has stood for nearly two millennia as a testament to Rome's ambition and ingenuity. But behind this awe-inspiring edifice lies a story of political maneuvering, social transformation, and the relentless pursuit of power. To truly understand the Colosseum's significance, we must first step back into the era that gave birth to it: the reign of the Flavian emperors.

The Flavian dynasty emerged from a period of unparalleled chaos, yet it became synonymous with stability and renewal. The Colosseum, the dynasty's crowning achievement, was more than just an architectural wonder; it was a declaration of intent. It was a gift to the people of Rome, a stage for imperial propaganda, and a symbol of the enduring legacy the Flavians sought to leave behind. Let us begin this chapter by exploring the rise of the dynasty that dared to dream of such a colossus.

The Rise of the Flavian Dynasty

The year was 69 CE, a time of chaos and uncertainty in the Roman Empire. Known as the Year of the Four Emperors, it saw a rapid succession of rulers vying for power, each falling victim to assassination, rebellion, or political intrigue. Out of this turbulence emerged a new dynasty—the Flavians—led by a pragmatic general named Vespasian. His ascent to power marked the beginning of a stabilizing era for Rome, one rooted in consolidation, infrastructure, and, perhaps most importantly, public goodwill.

Vespasian was not born into privilege. Unlike the Julio-Claudian emperors before him, who boasted divine ancestry, Vespasian's family hailed from modest origins in the Italian countryside. This background made him relatable to ordinary Romans, many of whom were weary of the excesses and corruption of previous regimes. But Vespasian was no ordinary man. He had proven his mettle as a military commander during the Roman conquest of Britain and the suppression of the Jewish revolt in Judea. By the time he claimed the title of emperor, he had not only earned the loyalty of the legions but also the trust of the Senate and the people.

The Flavian dynasty, which would span Vespasian's reign and that of his two sons, Titus and Domitian, was marked by a focus on practical governance and public works. Unlike the ostentatious Nero, whose infamous Golden House had drained Rome's coffers and alienated its citizens, the Flavians sought to rebuild the empire's finances and restore its moral fabric. Central to their strategy was the idea of creating monuments that would both celebrate Rome's power and serve its people. Enter the Colosseum, the most ambitious construction project of its time.

The Vision for the Colosseum: A Gift to the People

Vespasian's vision for the Colosseum was both grand and symbolic. He chose to build it on the site of Nero's Golden House, an opulent palace that had become a symbol of imperial excess and disconnect from the populace. By transforming this private playground of a despised emperor into a public arena, Vespasian sought to send a clear message: the Flavians were rulers of the people, not above them.

The Colosseum's construction began in 72 CE, financed in part by the spoils of the Jewish revolt. This was no ordinary building project; it was an architectural and engineering marvel designed to showcase the empire's wealth, ingenuity, and mastery over nature. The amphitheater would feature four levels of seating, accommodating up to 50,000 spectators, with designated areas for various social classes. Its design included advanced features such as a retractable awning (the velarium) to shield spectators from the sun and an underground network of tunnels (the hypogeum) for housing gladiators, animals, and stage equipment.

But the Colosseum was more than just a venue for entertainment; it was a tool of propaganda. The spectacles held within its walls—from gladiatorial combat to staged naval battles—were designed to awe and pacify the masses, reinforcing the emperor's divine authority. These games, often brutal and bloody, served as a reminder of Rome's might and the emperor's generosity. Free admission and free food distributed during the games ensured that the Colosseum became a beloved institution among the people.

The decision to name the amphitheater the Flavian Amphitheater (later known as the Colosseum due to its proximity to a colossal statue of Nero) was another nod to the dynasty's desire for lasting legacy. Vespasian never saw its completion; the arena was inaugurated by his son Titus in 80 CE with a 100-day spectacle that included gladiatorial contests, animal hunts, and mock naval battles. Titus' reign was brief but marked by this monumental achievement, cementing the Flavian dynasty's place in history.

The Colosseum, as a concept, was more than bricks and mortar; it was an embodiment of Rome's ambition. It stood as a testament to the city's architectural innovation and its rulers' ability to manipulate public perception. For the Flavians, the Colosseum was a means to erase the excesses of Nero's reign and rebuild the bond between the emperor and the people. It was, quite literally, a stage for their power.

Chapter 2:

Engineering Marvel: Building the Colosseum

The Colosseum, an enduring symbol of Rome's architectural brilliance, stands as a testament to the ingenuity and ambition of ancient engineers and builders. Constructed nearly two millennia ago, its imposing arches, towering walls, and intricate design continue to inspire awe. But what makes the Colosseum more extraordinary is not just its grandeur, but the innovative techniques, resourceful materials, and remarkable teamwork that brought this colossal structure to life.

Construction Techniques and Materials

Building the Colosseum was no ordinary feat. The scale and complexity of the project demanded techniques that were ahead of their time. The construction began under Emperor Vespasian in 72 CE and was completed in 80 CE during the reign of his son Titus, a remarkably short period for such an ambitious project.

At its core, the Colosseum's strength lies in its revolutionary use of concrete, a material perfected by Roman engineers. Unlike modern concrete, Roman concrete—a blend of lime, volcanic ash, and rubble—was incredibly durable and resistant to environmental damage. This innovation allowed the Colosseum to withstand earthquakes, floods, and the passage of time better than many later structures.

The outer walls, towering at approximately 157 feet, were constructed using travertine, a sturdy limestone quarried from Tivoli, about 20 miles from Rome. These stones were held together not with mortar but with iron clamps, providing flexibility and strength. For the inner structure, tufa, a softer volcanic stone, and brick-faced concrete were used to reduce weight while maintaining stability.

One of the Colosseum's most ingenious features was its series of arches, which provided structural integrity and allowed for the even distribution of weight. These arches not only supported the massive structure but also created a network of passageways and entrances, enabling the efficient movement of thousands of spectators.

Another remarkable innovation was the hypogeum, an underground labyrinth of tunnels and chambers. This area housed gladiators, animals, and stage equipment, making it possible to create elaborate spectacles.

Hydraulic mechanisms and trapdoors were incorporated, allowing for dramatic entrances and quick scene changes.

The velarium, a retractable awning, was yet another marvel. Made of canvas and operated by sailors from the Roman navy, it could be extended to provide shade for spectators. The engineering precision required to design and operate this feature highlights the Romans' mastery over both form and function.

The Masterminds: Architects, Engineers, and Workers

The construction of the Colosseum was a collaborative effort involving a diverse team of skilled individuals. While history has not preserved the names of the architects and engineers responsible for its design, their work speaks volumes about their expertise and vision.

Roman architects were meticulous planners, using advanced mathematical principles and design techniques to ensure the Colosseum's stability and functionality. Engineers oversaw the practical aspects, from transporting massive stones to erecting the towering walls. The precision required to fit the travertine blocks together without mortar was an extraordinary achievement.

Laborers, many of whom were slaves or prisoners of war, provided the muscle needed to bring the Colosseum to life. Their work was grueling, involving the transportation of heavy materials, carving stone, and assembling the massive structure. Skilled artisans added the finishing touches, including intricate carvings and decorative elements that showcased Rome's artistic prowess.

The workforce also included naval personnel, who operated the velarium. Their maritime expertise was essential for the complex system of ropes and pulleys used to deploy the awning. This collaboration between different groups underscores the Romans' ability to unite diverse talents for a common purpose.

A Timeline of Construction

The construction of the Colosseum unfolded in three main phases:

1. **72-75 CE: The Foundation and Outer Structure**
   The project began with the excavation of the site,

which had previously housed Nero's artificial lake. The drained area was filled with a solid foundation of concrete. Work on the outer walls and the first tier of arches commenced, using travertine blocks transported from Tivoli.

2. **75-78 CE: The Inner Structure and Hypogeum**
Once the outer walls were completed, attention shifted to the interior. The seating tiers were constructed using concrete and tufa, while the hypogeum began to take shape. This underground system was a feat of engineering, with its complex network of tunnels and chambers.

3. **78-80 CE: Final Touches and Inauguration**
During the final phase, finishing touches such as decorative elements and seating arrangements were completed. The velarium was installed, and the arena floor was prepared for its inaugural games. In 80 CE, Titus officially opened the Colosseum with a 100-day celebration featuring gladiatorial combat, animal hunts, and elaborate spectacles.

The Legacy of Construction

The Colosseum's construction set a benchmark for architectural and engineering excellence. It demonstrated the Romans' ability to combine functionality with aesthetic appeal, creating a structure that was not only practical but also visually stunning. The techniques pioneered during its construction influenced the design of amphitheaters and public buildings for centuries to come.

Chapter 3:

A Day in Ancient Rome: The Colosseum Unveiled

The year was 80 CE, and Rome was abuzz with anticipation. The Flavian Amphitheater, later known as the Colosseum, was finally complete. Citizens of all classes, from senators in their elegant togas to plebeians eager for entertainment, gathered for an event that promised to be as grand as the structure itself. Emperor Titus had declared a hundred days of games to celebrate the opening of this architectural marvel. The city's streets were alive with the sound of chatter, laughter, and the occasional roar of exotic beasts being transported to their fate.

The unveiling of the Colosseum was more than an event; it was a spectacle designed to solidify the Flavian dynasty's power and generosity in the minds of the Roman people. The amphitheater, with its towering arches and meticulous design, stood as a testament to Rome's ingenuity and ambition. This chapter takes you inside that historic day, a moment when Rome's might and magnificence were on full display.

The Grand Opening Games

The Colosseum's inaugural games were nothing short of a masterpiece of planning and execution. Over 100 days, tens of thousands of Romans would witness events that ranged from gladiatorial combat to mock naval battles. The first day, however, set the tone with unparalleled grandeur.

The morning began with the pompa, a grand procession led by Titus himself. Dressed in ceremonial garb, the emperor paraded through the streets, accompanied by priests, dignitaries, and performers. The procession was a feast for the senses: the scent of burning incense filled the air, musicians played triumphal hymns, and acrobats dazzled the crowds with their feats of skill. Behind them marched animals from the farthest reaches of the empire—lions, elephants, and even crocodiles—destined to meet their fate in the arena.

As the crowd settled into the Colosseum's seats, the sheer scale of the amphitheater became apparent. It could hold over 50,000 spectators, each with a clear view of the arena. The seating arrangement was a reflection of Rome's social hierarchy: senators occupied the best seats near the action, while women and the poor were relegated to the upper tiers. Despite these divisions, the crowd's excitement was universal. They were here to witness history.

The games began with venationes, wild animal hunts that showcased the bravery of hunters and the exotic wonders of Rome's empire. Leopards pounced, elephants charged, and the crowd roared with each dramatic moment. These hunts were not mere sport; they were a demonstration of Rome's dominion over nature, a theatrical reminder of the empire's vast reach.

As the day progressed, gladiators took center stage. Men of varying backgrounds—slaves, prisoners of war, and even volunteers—faced off in battles that combined skill, strategy, and spectacle. The crowd cheered for their favorites, and the emperor himself decided the fate of defeated combatants with a gesture of his hand. The tension and drama were palpable, and for many, this was the highlight of the day.

Perhaps the most astonishing part of the opening games was the naumachiae, or mock naval battles. Using a complex system of aqueducts, the arena floor was flooded, transforming it into a miniature sea. Ships manned by condemned prisoners clashed in a dramatic reenactment of famous naval engagements. The engineering required to achieve this feat left the audience in awe and cemented the Colosseum's reputation as a stage for the impossible.

Initial Reactions: Awe and Propaganda

The reaction to the Colosseum's unveiling was one of overwhelming awe. For many Romans, the amphitheater was unlike anything they had ever seen. Its massive size, intricate design, and the sheer variety of events it hosted were unparalleled. The people marveled at the retractable velarium, which shaded them from the sun, and the seamless organization of such a vast crowd.

But the games were more than entertainment; they were a calculated act of propaganda. The Flavian dynasty, still relatively new, used the Colosseum to solidify its legitimacy and win the favor of the people. By providing free games and distributing food, Titus positioned himself as a generous and benevolent ruler. The Colosseum's very existence—built on the site of Nero's despised Golden House—was a statement of the Flavians' commitment to the public good.

The events within the arena also reinforced Rome's power and unity. Gladiatorial games celebrated martial valor, while the venationes symbolized control over the natural world. Even the seating arrangement served as a reminder of the social order, with each citizen knowing their place in the grand hierarchy of the empire.

Chapter 4:

The Anatomy of an Arena

To truly appreciate the marvel that is the Colosseum, one must go beyond its towering arches and iconic silhouette. The Colosseum was not just an architectural feat but a meticulously planned space, designed to accommodate tens of thousands of spectators, stage breathtaking spectacles, and symbolize Rome's unparalleled mastery over engineering and design. From its seating arrangements to its ingenious hypogeum and the revolutionary velarium, every aspect of the Colosseum reflected a blend of functionality and grandeur. Moreover, its placement within the city's urban fabric tied it to the heart of Roman political and social life, making it more than an arena—it was a microcosm of Rome itself.

Design and Layout: Seating, Hypogeum, and Velarium

Seating: A Hierarchy in Stone

The Colosseum's seating arrangement was a testament to the Roman obsession with order and hierarchy. Its elliptical structure, stretching 189 meters long and 156 meters wide, could accommodate over 50,000 spectators. But who sat where was no arbitrary matter—it was a reflection of Rome's rigid social stratification.

At the lowest level, closest to the action, sat the senators. These elite individuals enjoyed marble seats with their names inscribed, offering them the best view of the spectacles. Just above them were the equestrians, Rome's wealthy class of knights, followed by the general citizenry in the middle tiers. The uppermost levels were reserved for the lower classes, including women and the poor. These wooden benches provided a view from afar, but for many, simply being inside the Colosseum was enough to feel connected to the grandeur of Rome.

The meticulous design ensured efficient crowd management. The Colosseum featured 80 entrances, known as vomitoria, which allowed the arena to be filled or emptied within minutes. This level of organization was unmatched, a precursor to modern stadium design.

The Hypogeum: A World Beneath the Arena

Beneath the Colosseum's sandy floor lay the hypogeum, an underground network of tunnels and chambers that brought the spectacles above to life. This subterranean marvel was a hub of activity, housing gladiators, exotic animals, and stage machinery. It was here that the drama of the games began, hidden from the audience's view.

The hypogeum featured a series of elevators and trapdoors operated by a complex system of pulleys and counterweights. These mechanisms allowed for sudden and dramatic appearances of gladiators or animals, adding an element of surprise to the spectacles. Lions could emerge roaring from beneath the sand, or an entire set could rise into view, transforming the arena in an instant. The ingenuity of the hypogeum's design showcased Roman engineering at its finest.

This underground world was also a place of tension and anticipation. Gladiators waited here, preparing for their moment in the spotlight, while handlers ensured that the animals were ready for their roles in the spectacle. The hypogeum was both a backstage and a battlefield, its shadows steeped in the anticipation of life-and-death drama.

The Velarium: Engineering Comfort

The Colosseum's velarium, a massive retractable awning, was a marvel of both engineering and practicality. Designed to shield spectators from the harsh Roman sun, the velarium was operated by sailors from the Roman navy, whose expertise with ropes and sails made them the ideal crew for this task.

The velarium consisted of a network of poles, ropes, and canvas that could be extended or retracted as needed. Its design allowed for ventilation, ensuring that spectators remained cool even during the height of summer. The fact that the Romans could achieve this level of comfort in a structure of such scale is a testament to their ingenuity and attention to detail.

The Colosseum in Context: The Forum and Roman Urban Design

The Colosseum was not an isolated structure; it was deeply integrated into the fabric of Rome. Built on the site of Nero's artificial lake, it symbolized the Flavian dynasty's commitment to the public good, reclaiming space that had once been reserved for imperial indulgence.

A Symbol of Renewal

The Colosseum's location was carefully chosen to reflect the Flavian emperors' vision. Situated near the Roman Forum, the political and economic heart of the city, the Colosseum became part of a broader narrative of renewal and accessibility. By placing the amphitheater in this central location, the Flavians made a statement: the excesses of Nero's reign were over, and Rome was once again a city for its people.

The Colosseum also connected to other significant landmarks, such as the Temple of Venus and Roma and the Arch of Constantine, creating a cohesive urban landscape that celebrated Rome's power and grandeur. Its proximity to these sites ensured that it was not just a venue for entertainment but also a part of the city's ceremonial and political life.

A Blueprint for the Empire

The design of the Colosseum influenced the construction of amphitheaters throughout the Roman Empire. From North Africa to Gaul, smaller versions of the Colosseum sprang up, each adapted to local needs but retaining the essence of its Roman prototype. This replication reinforced the cultural and political unity of the empire, making the Colosseum not just a Roman icon but a symbol of imperial identity.

SPECTACLE AND SOCIETY

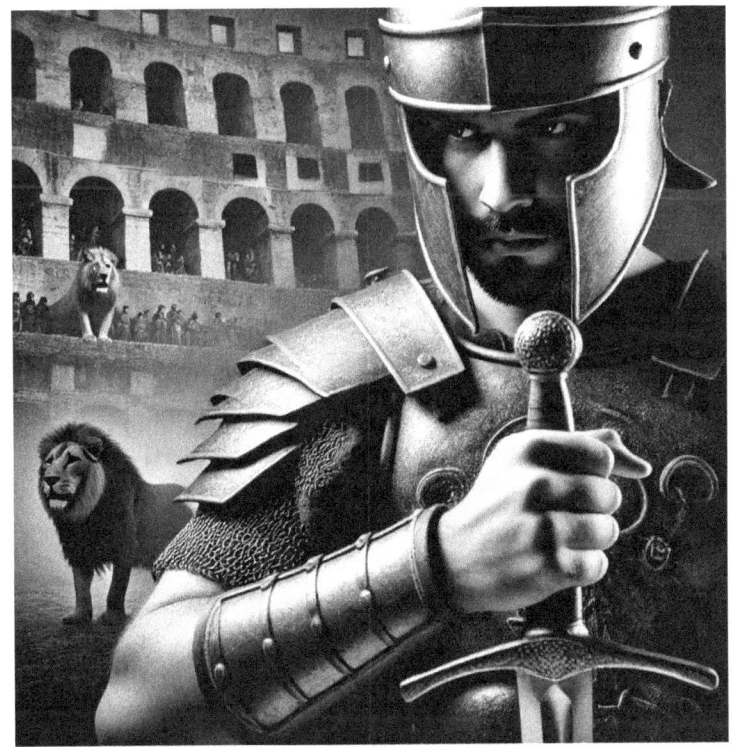

Chapter 5:

Entertaining the Masses: The Purpose of the Games

When the Colosseum roared with the sounds of clashing swords, roaring beasts, and cheering crowds, it became more than just an arena. It was a stage upon which the social, political, and cultural dynamics of ancient Rome played out. The games served as a mirror of Roman society, reflecting both its grandeur and its complexities. They were more than mere entertainment; they were tools of political control, a means of social cohesion, and a way for emperors to assert their power and legitimacy.

Bread, Circuses, and Political Control

The phrase "bread and circuses" (panem et circenses) comes from the Roman poet Juvenal, who used it to critique the way politicians distracted the populace from societal issues by providing free grain and grand spectacles. While Juvenal's words were biting, they also encapsulate a truth about Roman governance: the games were an effective strategy for maintaining public order.

In a city as vast and diverse as Rome, keeping the populace content was no small feat. The games served as a unifying force, drawing citizens from all walks of life to witness spectacles that reinforced their shared identity as Romans. By offering free admission and distributing food during events, the emperors ensured that even the poorest citizens could participate. This inclusivity fostered a sense of belonging and loyalty to the state.

The games also provided an outlet for the frustrations and grievances of the masses. In the controlled environment of the Colosseum, emotions ran high, but they were directed toward the action in the arena rather than the state. The thrilling displays of bravery and violence served as a catharsis for the crowd, diffusing tensions that might otherwise have boiled over into unrest.

But the games were not just about distraction; they were also about demonstrating Rome's power and dominance. The venationes, or wild animal hunts, showcased exotic creatures from across the empire—lions from Africa, tigers from Asia, and bears from Europe. These spectacles reminded the audience of Rome's vast reach and its ability to conquer and control the natural world. The gladiatorial combats celebrated martial valor and discipline, virtues that were central to Rome's identity as a military power.

The Role of Emperors in Shaping Spectacles

The games were also a powerful platform for imperial propaganda. Each emperor left his mark on the spectacles, using them to craft his public image and reinforce his authority. From the inaugural games held by Titus to the extravagant spectacles of Commodus, the Colosseum became a stage not just for combat but for the performance of power.

Titus: Generosity and Renewal

Titus, who inaugurated the Colosseum in 80 CE, used the games to solidify his reputation as a generous and benevolent ruler. The inaugural games lasted 100 days and featured a dazzling array of events, including gladiatorial contests, animal hunts, and mock naval battles. Titus' decision to provide free admission and distribute food to the crowd further cemented his image as a ruler who cared for his people. In a city still recovering from the devastation of the eruption of Mount Vesuvius and a major fire, the games were a way to lift the spirits of the populace and showcase the stability of the Flavian dynasty.

Domitian: Spectacle and Control

Titus' brother and successor, Domitian, took a different approach. While he continued the tradition of hosting games, he used them more explicitly as a tool for control. Domitian's games were known for their elaborate and sometimes grotesque nature, pushing the boundaries of spectacle to maintain the public's awe. He also expanded the role of women and dwarves in the games, breaking with tradition to captivate the audience's attention.

Domitian's spectacles served as a reminder of the emperor's power to both provide and punish. By staging public executions as part of the games, he reinforced the idea of justice being meted out by the state. The arena became a place where Rome's laws and values were dramatized for all to see.

Commodus: The Emperor as Gladiator

Perhaps no emperor's relationship with the games was as controversial as that of Commodus. Unlike his predecessors, who maintained a certain distance from the action, Commodus stepped into the arena himself. Dressed as Hercules, he fought as a gladiator, an act that shocked the Roman elite but thrilled the masses. While his participation was largely symbolic—his opponents were carefully chosen to ensure his victory—it blurred the lines between ruler and performer.

Commodus' antics may have diminished the dignity of the imperial office in the eyes of some, but they also underscored the games' power as a medium of connection. By participating directly, Commodus tapped into the crowd's adoration and used the arena to bolster his image as a hero and protector of Rome.

Chapter 6:

Gladiators: Heroes, Slaves, and Legends

The figure of the gladiator looms large in the imagination, a symbol of courage, skill, and defiance in the face of death. These warriors of the arena were both revered and reviled, celebrated as heroes yet often shackled by the chains of slavery. The life of a gladiator was one of paradoxes—a life of hardship and danger, but also one that offered the possibility of fame, fortune, and even freedom. Over centuries, the myths surrounding gladiators have only grown, shaped by figures like Spartacus and Commodus and reimagined through Hollywood's lens. To truly understand these iconic fighters, we must delve into the realities of their lives, their training, and their legacy.

The Life of a Gladiator: Training, Hierarchy, and Fame

Training: From Recruitment to Readiness

For many gladiators, their journey began not with a choice but with compulsion. Slaves, prisoners of war, and criminals were often condemned to the life of a gladiator as punishment. However, some men, and occasionally women, chose the path voluntarily, driven by desperation, debt, or the allure of potential glory. These voluntary gladiators, known as *auctorati*, signed contracts that outlined the terms of their service and the rewards they could earn.

Training took place in specialized schools known as *ludi*. These institutions were a mix of prison, barracks, and gymnasium, run by a *lanista*, the owner and manager of gladiators. The training regimen was grueling and unrelenting, designed to turn recruits into disciplined and skilled combatants. Gladiators practiced with wooden weapons heavier than those used in the arena, building their strength and endurance. They were taught not just how to fight, but how to entertain—victory was important, but so was spectacle.

Gladiators were categorized into various types based on their fighting style and equipment. The *retiarius*, armed with a trident and a net, relied on speed and agility, while the heavily armored *murmillo* wielded a sword and shield. Each type of gladiator had its own strengths and vulnerabilities, and matches were often arranged to pit contrasting styles against one another, creating a dramatic and unpredictable contest.

Hierarchy: The Gladiatorial Ladder

Within the world of gladiators, there was a hierarchy that determined status and opportunities. At the bottom were the *damnati ad gladium*, criminals sentenced to fight as a form of execution. These men were often poorly trained and stood little chance in the arena. Above them were the *novicii*, newly recruited gladiators still honing their skills.

The elite gladiators, known as *veterani*, were seasoned fighters who had survived numerous battles. Some even achieved the coveted status of *primus palus*, the highest rank in a gladiatorial school. These men enjoyed privileges such as better living conditions and greater respect from their peers and the audience.

For the most successful gladiators, fame was a tangible reward. Their names were cheered by the crowds, and their likenesses appeared on mosaics, graffiti, and even merchandise like oil lamps and coins. They could earn substantial sums of money and, in rare cases, their freedom. A gladiator who was granted the wooden sword, or *rudis*, was released from service and could live as a free citizen.

Fame and the Double-Edged Sword

Fame, however, was not without its challenges. While gladiators were celebrated by the public, they were often stigmatized by the Roman elite, who viewed them as little more than slaves or barbarians. Even freed gladiators faced social limitations, their past as fighters marking them as outsiders in Roman society.

Still, the allure of the arena was undeniable. For some, it was a path to redemption; for others, a chance to rise above their circumstances. In either case, the life of a gladiator was one of extremes, balancing peril with the promise of glory.

Myths and Realities: Spartacus, Commodus, and Hollywood's Impact

Spartacus: The Rebel Gladiator

No discussion of gladiators is complete without Spartacus, the most famous of them all. A Thracian warrior captured and sold into slavery, Spartacus trained as a gladiator before leading a massive slave revolt against Rome in 73 BCE. His rebellion, known as the

Third Servile War, saw tens of thousands of slaves rise up in a desperate bid for freedom.

Though ultimately defeated, Spartacus became a symbol of resistance and defiance. His story has been romanticized over the centuries, particularly in modern portrayals like the 1960 film *Spartacus*. While historical accounts are limited and often biased, the essence of Spartacus's legacy endures: a man who dared to challenge an empire.

Commodus: The Emperor as Gladiator

While Spartacus represents the nobility of rebellion, Commodus exemplifies the decadence of power. The son of Emperor Marcus Aurelius, Commodus shocked Rome by participating in gladiatorial combat himself. Dressed as Hercules, he fought in the arena, though his contests were carefully staged to ensure his safety.

Commodus' antics drew scorn from the Roman elite, who viewed his behavior as beneath the dignity of an emperor. Yet, for the masses, his appearances in the Colosseum were a thrilling spectacle. Commodus' reign is often remembered as a turning point in Roman history, marking the decline of the empire's stability and values.

Hollywood's Gladiators: Fact and Fiction

The modern image of the gladiator owes much to Hollywood, where films like *Gladiator* (2000) have immortalized these warriors as noble and heroic figures. While these portrayals capture the drama and intensity of the arena, they often blur the line between fact and fiction.

For instance, the depiction of gladiators as free-spirited rebels who fought against oppression oversimplifies their reality. Most gladiators were bound by their circumstances, their lives dictated by the whims of their owners and the demands of the audience. Additionally, the notion of gladiators fighting for abstract ideals like justice or freedom is more a product of modern storytelling than historical fact.

That said, Hollywood has succeeded in reigniting interest in the gladiatorial world, inspiring audiences to learn more about the true history behind the legends. The blend of myth and reality ensures that gladiators remain a fascinating subject, their legacy evolving with each retelling.

The Enduring Legacy of Gladiators

Gladiators occupy a unique place in history, embodying both the brutality and the brilliance of ancient Rome.

Their lives were shaped by violence, yet they achieved a form of immortality through their feats in the arena. From Spartacus's rebellion to Commodus' theatrics, and from ancient mosaics to modern films, gladiators continue to captivate our imagination, reminding us of the enduring allure of courage and spectacle.

Chapter 7:

Beasts in the Arena: Venationes and Beyond

The Colosseum's roars weren't just the sounds of gladiators clashing swords or crowds erupting with cheers; they were also the echoes of wild animals—exotic, fierce, and magnificent—brought from the farthest reaches of the Roman Empire to fight, entertain, and die. These venationes, or beast hunts, were among the most thrilling spectacles of the Roman games, showcasing the empire's dominion over nature and its ability to harness the wildest creatures for the amusement of its citizens. The involvement of animals in the arena was a testament to Roman ingenuity, cruelty, and flair for spectacle, providing an unparalleled window into their values and ambitions.

Wild Animals: Importation, Training, and Use in Games

A Menagerie from the Ends of the Earth

The Roman fascination with wild animals knew no bounds. The beasts featured in venationes were not just ordinary animals; they were the most exotic and fearsome creatures the empire could procure. Lions and leopards from North Africa, tigers from India, elephants from the subcontinent, bears from the forests of Europe, and crocodiles from the Nile all made their way to the Colosseum. These animals symbolized the vast reach of Rome's power, each one a trophy of imperial conquest.

Importing these creatures was no small feat. The process involved an intricate network of hunters, trappers, and traders who scoured the empire's frontiers for suitable specimens. Once captured, the animals were transported across great distances, often enduring weeks or months in cages aboard ships or carts. The logistics of such an operation were staggering; the Roman Empire essentially built a supply chain for wild beasts.

Upon arrival in Rome, these animals were housed in specially constructed menageries. These facilities were not just holding pens; they were training grounds where handlers, or *bestiarii*, acclimated the animals to human interaction and prepared them for their roles in the games. Training a beast for the arena was a dangerous and delicate task. The goal was not to tame the animal but to ensure that it behaved predictably under the chaos of the arena's bright lights, roaring crowds, and unfamiliar stimuli.

Roles in the Games

Animals in the Colosseum served a variety of purposes. In some venationes, hunters armed with spears and bows faced off against these creatures in a test of skill and courage. In others, the animals were set loose on condemned prisoners, their deaths serving as both punishment and entertainment. Occasionally, animals were pitted against each other in brutal fights, such as a lion versus a bear or a tiger versus a bull. These contests were carefully staged to maximize drama and audience engagement.

But not all animals were there to fight. Some were part of elaborate theatrical productions, their presence adding an exotic flair to mythological reenactments or processions. Elephants might carry performers dressed as gods, while leopards prowled the stage in scenes depicting distant lands. In every case, the animals' involvement underscored Rome's power—its ability to capture and command the untamable.

The Spectacle of Death: Animal vs. Gladiator

The Role of Bestiarii

Among the most dramatic events involving animals were the battles between beasts and gladiators, specifically the *bestiarii*. Unlike the more celebrated gladiators who fought other men, the bestiarii specialized in facing wild animals. Armed with spears, nets, or even just daggers, these fighters were tasked with subduing or killing their animal opponents in front of thousands of spectators.

The bestiarii's battles were brutal and highly dangerous. While some of them were trained professionals, many were slaves or condemned criminals forced into the role as a form of punishment. For these unfortunate individuals, survival depended on both skill and luck. Even the most experienced bestiarii knew that a single misstep could mean a swift and violent death.

These contests were not just about survival; they were about spectacle. A bestiarius who displayed courage, agility, and skill could earn the crowd's admiration, transforming what might have been a death sentence into a path to glory. The audience's reactions—their gasps, cheers, and cries for blood—were as much a part of the spectacle as the combat itself.

The Psychology of the Spectacle

The sight of a man facing off against a wild animal tapped into deep-seated emotions for the Roman audience. It was a display of human dominance over nature, a celebration of bravery, and a reminder of the thin line between life and death. For the spectators, it was also a cathartic experience. Watching a man overcome a lion or be trampled by an elephant allowed the crowd to confront their own fears and mortality from the safety of their seats.

At the same time, these spectacles raised questions about humanity's capacity for cruelty. Even in ancient Rome, some voices criticized the games for their brutality. The philosopher Seneca, for instance, decried the venationes as a display of senseless violence, though such critiques did little to dampen the public's enthusiasm.

Chapter 8:

Sea Battles and Set Pieces: Beyond Gladiatorial Combat

The Colosseum, though famous for its gladiatorial combats and beast hunts, was also the stage for some of the most extraordinary spectacles the ancient world had ever seen. Among these were the *naumachiae*, or staged naval battles, and the lavish set pieces that transformed the arena into a fantastical world of myth and wonder. These productions went far beyond simple entertainment; they were showcases of Roman engineering, artistry, and imperial power. In this chapter, we dive into the fascinating world of naval battles and elaborate productions that pushed the boundaries of imagination and technology.

Naumachiae: Staging Naval Battles in the Arena

Turning Sand into Sea

One of the most ambitious spectacles ever staged in the Colosseum was the *naumachia*, a mock naval battle that transformed the sandy arena floor into a miniature sea. The logistics of such an event were staggering. The Colosseum's underground hypogeum, a complex network of tunnels and chambers, could be flooded using a sophisticated system of aqueducts and drains. Within hours, the arena floor was transformed into a water-filled basin, capable of hosting small ships and their crews.

These battles were not merely symbolic or ceremonial; they were dramatic recreations of historical naval conflicts or mythological sea battles. Participants, often prisoners or condemned criminals, fought to the death, adding a grim authenticity to the spectacle. The ships themselves were replicas of Roman and enemy vessels, complete with masts, sails, and oars, designed to give the audience a realistic portrayal of naval warfare.

The Drama of Battle

The *naumachiae* were carefully choreographed to maximize drama and engagement. Crews of oarsmen and fighters battled on miniature seas, their movements mirroring real-life naval tactics. Ramming, boarding, and hand-to-hand combat played out as the audience cheered and jeered. The addition of archers firing flaming arrows and pyrotechnic effects heightened the spectacle, turning the Colosseum into a theater of chaos and excitement.

The scale of these events was monumental. During the inaugural games of the Colosseum in 80 CE, Emperor Titus is said to have staged a *naumachia* involving thousands of participants and several dozen ships. These battles were not only a testament to Rome's engineering prowess but also a demonstration of imperial wealth and power. They reminded the audience of Rome's naval supremacy and its ability to dominate both land and sea.

Extravagant Productions: Scenery, Sets, and Special Effects

Transforming the Arena

While the *naumachiae* showcased the Colosseum's ability to become a sea, other productions transformed it into lush forests, mythical landscapes, and even celestial realms. These set pieces were integral to theatrical reenactments of famous myths, historical events, and legendary tales. Using a combination of natural materials, painted backdrops, and movable platforms, the arena became an ever-changing stage.

The Colosseum's hypogeum played a crucial role in these transformations. Trapdoors and elevators allowed for sudden appearances of actors, animals, or props. Entire trees could be hoisted into the arena to create a forest, while massive structures such as temples or ships could rise from beneath the floor. This dynamic stagecraft created a sense of wonder and unpredictability, ensuring that every event felt unique and unforgettable

Special Effects and Illusions

The Romans were masters of theatrical illusion, and their special effects rivaled those of modern productions. Pyrotechnics were used to simulate lightning, fire, and explosions, while mirrors and polished metals created dazzling light displays. Artificial rain, fog, and even snow were produced to enhance the realism of scenes, immersing the audience in the drama.

Mythological reenactments often included appearances by gods and heroes, who would descend from the arena's upper levels on mechanical cranes known as *machinae*. These devices allowed actors to "fly" across the arena, creating moments of awe and surprise. Combined with music, chants, and the roar of the crowd, these productions were immersive experiences that transported the audience into another world.

The Spectacle of Myth and Legend

Some of the most memorable set pieces were drawn from Roman and Greek mythology. Tales of Hercules, Perseus, and the Trojan War were brought to life with an attention to detail that blurred the line between reality and fantasy. For example, a reenactment of the Labors of Hercules might feature the hero slaying the Nemean lion, with both man and beast emerging dramatically from beneath the arena floor. Similarly, the story of Perseus rescuing Andromeda from the sea monster Cetus could be staged using elaborate water effects and mechanical creatures.

These productions were more than mere entertainment; they were cultural touchstones that reinforced Rome's connection to the classical past and its claim to the mantle of civilization. By dramatizing these stories, the Romans celebrated their heritage and reminded the audience of their place in a grand, mythic narrative.

The Message Behind the Spectacle

The *naumachiae* and set pieces of the Colosseum were not just feats of engineering and artistry; they were tools of imperial propaganda. These grand spectacles reinforced the idea that Rome was the center of the world, a place where even the elements could be controlled for the enjoyment of its citizens. The ability to stage such events demonstrated the emperor's power and generosity, securing his place in the hearts of the people.

Yet, these spectacles also hinted at the fragility of this power. The immense resources and labor required to produce them were a reminder of the empire's dependence on its vast territories and subjugated peoples. For all their splendor, the *naumachiae* and theatrical productions were fleeting, their grandeur lasting only as long as the applause of the crowd.

BEHIND THE SCENES

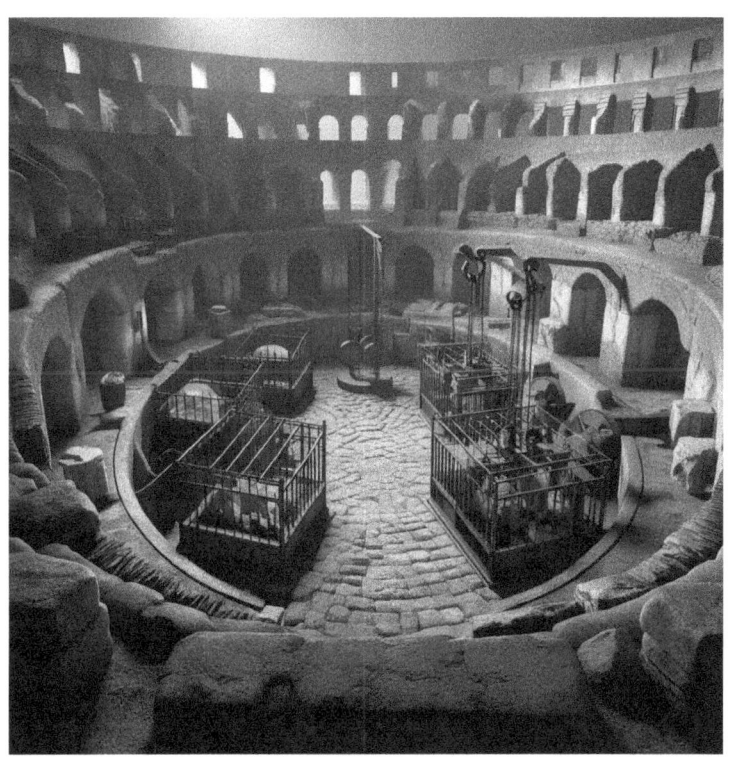

Chapter 9:

The Logistics of Spectacle

Behind the grandeur and spectacle of the Colosseum lay an intricate and highly organized machine. The games that thrilled the masses were not spontaneous displays of chaos; they were meticulously planned productions that required extraordinary logistical effort. From managing resources to ensuring the comfort of tens of thousands of spectators, the logistics of spectacle reveal a side of the Colosseum that often goes unnoticed: the human ingenuity and effort that made such monumental events possible.

Organizing Games: Planning, Resources, and Execution

The Planning Phase

Organizing games in the Colosseum was akin to producing a modern blockbuster event. The process began long before the first trumpet sounded. Roman officials, often in collaboration with the emperor, determined the scope and scale of the games. Would it be a week of standard gladiatorial combat, or a month-long extravaganza featuring naval battles, exotic animal hunts, and theatrical reenactments? Once the vision was set, the real work began.

Securing participants was one of the first steps. Gladiators were recruited from *ludi gladiatorii* (gladiator schools), while prisoners and condemned criminals were selected to fill the ranks of combatants and animal fodder. For grander events, wild animals were imported from the farthest reaches of the empire, necessitating complex coordination with hunters, trappers, and transporters. These animals often included lions, tigers, elephants, and even crocodiles, all of which had to be captured, transported, and housed in Rome before the games began.

The games also required weapons, armor, and other props. Blacksmiths and craftsmen were commissioned to produce and maintain the necessary equipment. Specialized artisans created elaborate set pieces, from replica ships for naval battles to mechanical creatures for mythological reenactments. Every detail was accounted for to ensure a seamless and awe-inspiring performance.

Execution: The Day of the Games

On the day of the event, a highly organized team ensured that everything ran smoothly. The *editor*, or producer of the games (often an emperor or a wealthy sponsor), oversaw the proceedings, though much of the work was delegated to a network of officials and slaves. The *praefectus annonae*, responsible for Rome's grain supply, coordinated the distribution of food to the spectators, while the *aquaeductarii* managed the water supply, including the intricate systems used to flood the arena for naval battles.

The games followed a carefully planned schedule, with events arranged to build excitement throughout the day. Morning sessions typically featured animal hunts and executions, followed by gladiatorial contests in the afternoon. Grand finale events, such as mock naval battles or mythological dramas, were reserved for the evening when the crowd's anticipation had reached its peak.

Behind the scenes, a vast workforce ensured the smooth execution of each event. Gladiators and performers awaited their cues in the hypogeum, while handlers managed the animals, ensuring they were ready for their dramatic entrances. Musicians and announcers coordinated their performances to heighten the drama, providing a soundtrack to the spectacle.

Feeding the Arena: Food, Water, and Waste Management

Sustaining the Crowd

The Colosseum could accommodate over 50,000 spectators, and feeding such a massive crowd was no small task. Vendors roamed the stands selling bread, olives, fruit, and wine, much like modern stadium vendors hawking hotdogs and beer. Free grain distributions, part of the Roman welfare system, were often timed to coincide with major events, ensuring that even the poorest citizens could enjoy the games without going hungry.

In addition to food, wine was a staple of the Roman entertainment experience. Amphorae of wine were transported to the Colosseum and distributed through a network of vendors. The challenge of serving thousands of spectators in an orderly fashion required careful planning and an army of workers.

Managing Water

Water management was another critical component of the Colosseum's logistics. The aqueducts that supplied Rome with fresh water were also used to meet the needs of the Colosseum. Drinking fountains and basins were strategically placed throughout the structure to keep spectators hydrated. In the case of *naumachiae*, the arena floor could be flooded with water transported through a network of pipes and sluices. Once the event was over, the water was drained just as efficiently, leaving the arena ready for the next spectacle.

Waste Disposal: The Hidden Operation

With thousands of spectators, performers, and animals in one place, waste management was an inevitable and challenging task. The Colosseum's design included features to address this issue. A system of drains and sewers removed liquid waste, while a dedicated workforce of slaves and laborers cleared solid debris from the stands and arena floor.

Animal waste from the hypogeum was a particular challenge, especially during events involving exotic creatures. Handlers and cleaners worked tirelessly to ensure that the stench and mess were kept under control, preserving the atmosphere of the event.

The Unseen Heroes of the Colosseum

The success of the Colosseum's games depended on the labor of thousands of unseen individuals. From the artisans who crafted armor and props to the slaves who cleaned the arena, these workers were the backbone of Rome's entertainment machine. Their efforts ensured that the grandeur of the games remained unblemished by logistical failures, allowing the audience to focus on the spectacle before them.

Chapter 10:

The Economy of the Colosseum

The Colosseum, with its towering arches and roaring crowds, was more than just a stage for blood and spectacle; it was an economic engine. Behind every gladiatorial combat and wild beast hunt lay a complex web of financial transactions, investments, and profits. The games were a testament to Rome's ability to turn spectacle into a lucrative enterprise, benefitting everyone from emperors to humble vendors. This chapter explores the economic mechanics that powered the Colosseum, uncovering the immense costs of staging such spectacles and the diverse network of individuals and institutions that profited from them.

The Financial Cost of Spectacle

Building the Colosseum

Before the first games could even take place, the Colosseum itself represented a monumental investment. Commissioned by Emperor Vespasian in 72 CE and completed by his sons Titus and Domitian, the amphitheater was a gift to the Roman people—but it was also a statement of power and ambition. Constructed with high-quality travertine stone, marble, and concrete, the Colosseum's materials were sourced from across the empire. The sheer scale of the project demanded vast sums of money, a workforce of thousands (many of whom were slaves or prisoners of war), and years of coordinated effort.

The funding for the Colosseum's construction reportedly came from the spoils of the Jewish War, including the sack of Jerusalem in 70 CE. This use of plunder underscored the amphitheater's dual purpose: it was both a place of public entertainment and a monument to Roman military supremacy.

Staging the Games

Once the Colosseum was built, the cost of hosting games became an ongoing financial burden. Staging even a single day of events required significant resources. Gladiators had to be trained and equipped; wild animals had to be captured, transported, and fed; and the arena itself had to be prepared with sand, props, and sometimes elaborate set pieces. For special occasions, the costs could skyrocket. Naval battles (*naumachiae*) alone required the flooding of the arena and the construction of ships, not to mention the crews to man them.

The inaugural games held by Emperor Titus in 80 CE provide an example of the immense expenses involved. Lasting 100 days, these games featured gladiatorial contests, beast hunts, and mock naval battles. Thousands of animals were slaughtered, and countless participants fought in the arena, all at an enormous cost to the imperial treasury. Yet, for the Flavian dynasty, these expenses were justified. The games were a means of securing public favor and reinforcing the emperor's image as a generous and powerful ruler.

Ongoing Maintenance

The Colosseum itself required regular maintenance, from repairing its stonework to ensuring the functionality of its complex systems, such as the hypogeum's elevators and trapdoors. These ongoing costs were shouldered by the imperial administration, which treated the amphitheater as a vital public asset. Ensuring the Colosseum's continued operation was as much about sustaining its economic impact as it was about preserving its cultural significance.

Who Profited? Sponsors, Vendors, and Gladiator Schools

Sponsors: The Patrons of Spectacle

While emperors often financed major games, they were not the only ones footing the bill. Wealthy citizens and officials frequently sponsored smaller events as a way to gain prestige and political influence. By funding games, these patrons earned the admiration of the public, strengthening their social standing and political careers. The more extravagant the games, the greater the sponsor's reputation—though this could also lead to financial ruin if the costs spiraled out of control.

The *editor*, or producer of the games, was the individual responsible for overseeing their organization and funding. For an emperor, the games were a way to demonstrate benevolence and authority. For other sponsors, they were a calculated investment in their personal brand, offering both immediate applause and long-term social capital.

Vendors: Feeding the Spectators

The Colosseum's bustling crowds created a thriving marketplace. Vendors selling food, drinks, and souvenirs were a ubiquitous presence in and around the amphitheater. Spectators could purchase bread, olives, figs, and wine from hawkers who navigated the stands, much like modern-day concession vendors at sports arenas. Others set up stalls outside the Colosseum, catering to the tens of thousands of people who flocked to the games.

These vendors paid fees for the right to operate within the Colosseum's premises, generating additional revenue for the administrators. The bustling commerce around the games turned the Colosseum into not just a cultural hub but also an economic one, benefitting local producers and merchants.

Gladiator Schools: Training and Business

Gladiators, the stars of the Colosseum, were the products of a thriving industry. Gladiator schools (*ludi*) were both training centers and profitable businesses. Run by *lanistae*, these schools invested heavily in acquiring, training, and maintaining fighters. Slaves, prisoners of war, and volunteers (*auctorati*) were trained in combat techniques, fitness, and stagecraft to prepare them for the arena.

The *lanista* profited by leasing their gladiators to game sponsors, earning fees based on the fighters' skill levels and popularity. Elite gladiators, those who had achieved fame through numerous victories, commanded higher fees and attracted larger crowds. Some gladiators even became lucrative advertising tools, with their names and images appearing on merchandise such as oil lamps and mosaics.

However, running a gladiator school was not without risks. High mortality rates among fighters and the constant need for new recruits made the business precarious. Yet, for successful *lanistae*, the rewards were substantial, securing their place in the complex economy of the games.

The Economy of Spectacle

The Colosseum's economy was multifaceted, involving a wide range of participants and beneficiaries. From emperors and wealthy patrons to humble vendors and gladiator trainers, the amphitheater supported a vast network of economic activity. At its core, the games represented a unique intersection of entertainment, politics, and commerce, where every roar of the crowd echoed with the sound of coins changing hands.

Chapter 11:

Voices from the Past: Spectators and Participants

The Colosseum was not just a monument of stone and spectacle; it was a living, breathing stage where the stories of countless individuals unfolded. For the spectators, the games offered excitement, camaraderie, and a fleeting escape from the routines of Roman life. For the participants, however—the gladiators, slaves, and even the elite—it was a place of immense risk and reward, a space where their fate could be decided in the blink of an eye. This chapter delves into the diverse perspectives of those who experienced the Colosseum, from the roaring stands to the sandy arena floor.

The Experience of Watching the Games

The Atmosphere in the Stands

Imagine walking through one of the Colosseum's grand arches, past the bustling vendors selling bread, olives, and wine. The aroma of roasted meats mingles with the scent of sweat and sand as tens of thousands of spectators find their seats. The hum of conversation and laughter fills the air, punctuated by the occasional roar of anticipation as a lion's growl echoes from the arena below.

The Colosseum was a social microcosm, with its seating arrangement reflecting the rigid hierarchy of Roman society. Senators and other elite citizens occupied the best seats closest to the action, complete with marble benches and shade from the velarium. Above them sat the equestrians, followed by the general populace in the middle tiers. At the very top, women, slaves, and the poorest Romans crowded onto wooden benches, their view distant but their excitement no less palpable.

For the spectators, the games were a feast for the senses. The sight of gleaming armor and ferocious beasts, the sound of clashing weapons and the roar of the crowd, and even the tactile experience of throwing coins or bread to their favorite gladiators all combined to create an immersive experience. The games were not just entertainment; they were a collective ritual that reinforced the values and identity of Roman society.

Emotional Engagement

The crowd's emotions ebbed and flowed with the action in the arena. A skilled gladiator's deft maneuver could elicit a collective gasp, followed by thunderous applause. A misstep or brutal injury might provoke groans of sympathy or bloodthirsty cheers, depending on the crowd's mood. The emperor's role in deciding the fate of defeated gladiators added another layer of drama. Would the defeated fighter earn mercy and live to fight another day, or would the emperor's thumb turn downward, sealing their doom?

The audience's engagement was not passive; they actively participated in the games, chanting for their favorite fighters and demanding ever more extravagant spectacles. In a society where power and spectacle were intertwined, the Colosseum's games provided an outlet for the emotions and aspirations of Rome's citizens.

Personal Accounts of Gladiators, Slaves, and the Elite

The Gladiators: Heroes and Pawns

For the gladiators, the Colosseum was both a stage and a battlefield. Many of them were slaves or prisoners of war, forced into a life of combat. Yet, others chose this path voluntarily, lured by the promise of fame, fortune, and, in rare cases, freedom. Their lives were a mix of grueling training, camaraderie, and constant danger.

Gladiators often became the darlings of the crowd. Popular fighters were celebrated with graffiti, mosaics, and even songs. Yet, this fame came at a cost. The threat of death was ever-present, and even a victorious gladiator could suffer life-threatening injuries. Despite this, some gladiators spoke of the arena with pride, viewing it as a place where they could prove their skill and earn the respect of the masses.

One anonymous inscription from a retired gladiator reads: "I was once the master of the sand, a slave to none but the gods. In the arena, I found glory and freedom." Such accounts reveal the complex relationship gladiators had with their role in society, both as symbols of Roman virtues and as individuals caught in a brutal system.

The Slaves: Hidden Laborers

For the slaves who toiled behind the scenes, the Colosseum represented a different kind of struggle. These individuals were the lifeblood of the games, managing the animals, preparing the arena, and tending to the gladiators. Their contributions were largely invisible to the audience, yet without them, the spectacles would not have been possible.

Personal accounts from slaves are rare, but archaeological evidence and historical records provide glimpses into their lives. Inscriptions and graffiti left by slaves sometimes express frustration, defiance, or even humor. One slave's carving reads: "They roar for the lion, but not for the one who feeds it." Such words remind us of the humanity behind the machinery of spectacle, where even the voiceless found ways to leave their mark.

The Elite: Patrons and Spectators

For Rome's elite, the Colosseum was a place to see and be seen. Senators and equestrians attended the games not only for entertainment but also to reinforce their status. Their seats, located closest to the action, symbolized their importance in Roman society. For them, the games were as much about networking and political maneuvering as they were about enjoying the spectacle.

Some members of the elite were more directly involved in the games. Wealthy patrons often sponsored events, earning public favor and prestige. The emperor himself played a central role, presiding over the games and making life-or-death decisions about defeated combatants. For the elite, the Colosseum was not just an amphitheater; it was a stage for power and influence.

The writings of Roman senators and philosophers offer insights into their perspectives on the games. While some, like Cicero, viewed the games as a celebration of Roman virtues, others, such as Seneca, criticized their brutality. Seneca's letters describe the games as a moral quandary, a place where humanity's capacity for cruelty was laid bare. These conflicting views reflect the complexity of the Colosseum's role in Roman culture, both as a source of pride and as a point of contention.

The Human Stories of the Colosseum

The Colosseum was a place where lives intersected in dramatic and often tragic ways. Spectators and participants alike were drawn into its orbit, their experiences shaped by the grand spectacle of the games. From the roaring stands to the blood-soaked sand, the voices of the past echo through the Colosseum, reminding us of the human stories that gave it life.

Chapter 12:

The Ethical Dilemma of Roman Entertainment

The Colosseum—a grand stage for epic spectacles and a testament to Roman ingenuity—was also a place of unimaginable suffering. While the games brought joy and unity to Roman society, they also exposed the empire's darker side: its capacity for cruelty and its appetite for violence. From the voices of ancient critics to the reflections of modern society, the ethical dilemmas of Roman entertainment have long been a subject of debate. This chapter delves into these moral quandaries, exploring both the contemporary critiques of the games and their resonance in today's discussions on ethics, violence, and society.

Contemporary Criticism: Voices Against the Games

Philosophers and Morality

While the games were widely celebrated, not everyone in ancient Rome embraced them. Philosophers and intellectuals, particularly those influenced by Stoic and early Christian thought, often criticized the spectacles for their brutality and moral decay. One of the most vocal critics was Seneca the Younger, a Stoic philosopher and advisor to Emperor Nero. In his letters, Seneca condemned the gladiatorial games as a debasement of human dignity, describing them as a place where "killing is a pastime and men's blood is the entertainment."

Seneca's critique extended beyond the arena's violence; he saw the games as a reflection of society's moral decline. He lamented how the crowds reveled in the suffering of others, arguing that such spectacles desensitized people to cruelty and eroded their capacity for empathy. For Seneca, the games were not just entertainment—they were a symptom of a deeper societal sickness.

Early Christian Perspectives

Early Christians also voiced strong opposition to the games, viewing them as incompatible with their faith's teachings on compassion and the sanctity of life. Tertullian, an early Christian theologian, wrote extensively about the immorality of the arena. In his treatise *De Spectaculis*, Tertullian argued that the games glorified violence and idolatry, urging Christians to abstain from attending.

The Christian critique of the games was not purely moral; it was also spiritual. For Christians, the Colosseum's emphasis on death and violence clashed with their belief in redemption and the value of every human soul. Over time, as Christianity gained prominence in the Roman Empire, these criticisms contributed to the eventual decline of gladiatorial games.

Voices from the Margins

While much of the criticism of the games came from philosophers and religious leaders, other voices—though less well-documented—likely existed among the oppressed and enslaved. The prisoners and gladiators forced into the arena, as well as the slaves who toiled behind the scenes, must have viewed the games with a mixture of dread and resentment. Although their perspectives are largely absent from the historical record, graffiti, inscriptions, and artifacts offer glimpses of their resistance and humanity.

Modern Reflections: Ethics, Violence, and Society

The Parallels to Modern Entertainment

Though the Colosseum's games are firmly rooted in the past, their ethical questions resonate in the present. Modern society may not stage gladiatorial combat, but the appeal of violence as entertainment endures. From boxing and mixed martial arts to action films and violent video games, the boundaries between acceptable and exploitative entertainment remain contested.

The question of consent often arises in these debates. Unlike Roman gladiators, modern athletes and performers choose to participate in potentially dangerous activities. Yet, critics argue that even voluntary participation can be exploitative, particularly when economic pressures or societal expectations influence these choices. This echoes the plight of some *auctorati* in ancient Rome, who volunteered to become gladiators out of desperation or poverty.

Desensitization and Empathy

The ethical concerns raised by Seneca and Tertullian—that witnessing violence desensitizes people to suffering—are as relevant today as they were in ancient Rome. Studies on media and entertainment suggest that prolonged exposure to violent imagery can reduce empathy and normalize aggression. The Colosseum's games, with their blood-soaked sands and cheering crowds, offer a stark historical example of how entertainment can shape societal attitudes toward violence.

At the same time, some argue that confronting violence through art and entertainment can serve a cathartic or educational purpose. Films like *Gladiator* (2000) explore the brutality of the arena while inviting viewers to reflect on themes of power, morality, and humanity. This duality mirrors the Colosseum itself—a place of both awe-inspiring spectacle and profound moral ambiguity.

Society's Role in Spectacle

The Colosseum also raises questions about society's complicity in entertainment that exploits or endangers others. In ancient Rome, the games were a collective experience, with the crowd's reactions driving the events in the arena. Modern parallels can be found in reality television, viral internet challenges, and sports scandals, where audience demand often perpetuates unethical practices.

Reflecting on the Colosseum's legacy, it becomes clear that the ethical dilemmas of entertainment are deeply intertwined with societal values. What a culture chooses to celebrate or ignore speaks volumes about its priorities and principles.

DECLINE AND TRANSFORMATION

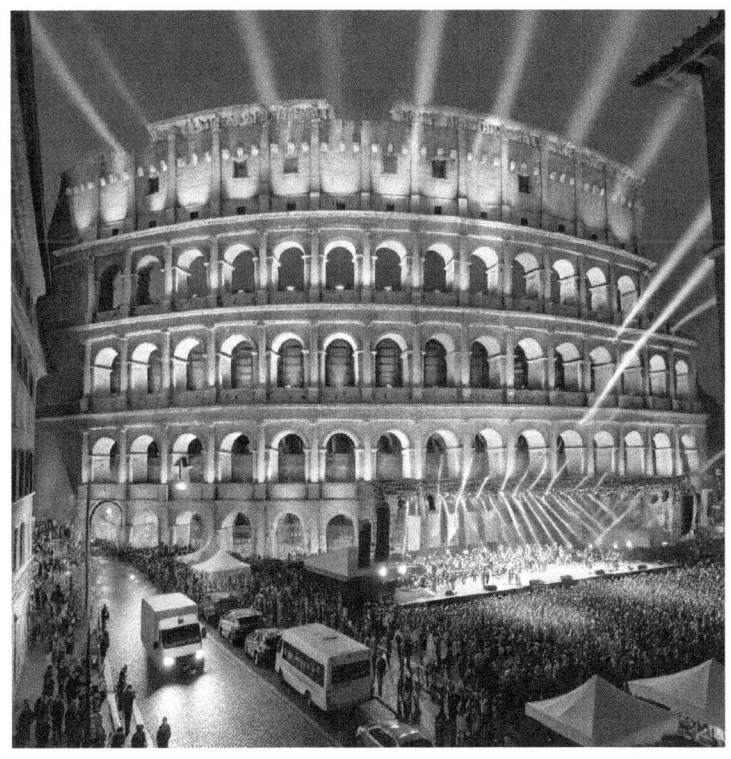

Chapter 13:

The Colosseum's Fall: Rome's Changing Landscape

The Colosseum, once the crowning jewel of Roman entertainment, has endured centuries of change, standing as a testament to the passage of time and the transformation of Rome itself. From its bustling days as an amphitheater to its gradual decline into ruin, the Colosseum's story mirrors the shifting fortunes of the empire that built it. This chapter explores the end of the gladiatorial games and the forces—natural and human—that led to the Colosseum's fall from glory.

The End of the Gladiatorial Games

Cultural and Political Shifts

The decline of the gladiatorial games was not an abrupt event but a gradual shift influenced by changing cultural, religious, and political dynamics. By the 4th century CE, the Roman Empire was undergoing significant transformations. The rise of Christianity as the dominant religion played a pivotal role in reshaping societal values. Gladiatorial combat, with its emphasis on violence and death, increasingly came into conflict with Christian teachings on compassion and the sanctity of life.

Emperor Constantine the Great, the first Roman emperor to convert to Christianity, issued reforms that began to limit the games. In 325 CE, he declared an end to the practice of sentencing criminals to gladiatorial combat, signaling the beginning of the end for the tradition. Although the games persisted in some form for several decades, they were gradually marginalized.

In 404 CE, Emperor Honorius officially banned gladiatorial combat following the death of a Christian monk, Telemachus, who was reportedly killed while trying to stop a fight in the arena. This event, whether historical or apocryphal, became a symbolic moment marking the end of an era. By the 6th century, gladiatorial games had faded into history, replaced by chariot races and other forms of public entertainment more aligned with the empire's evolving identity.

The Loss of Public Utility

As the games dwindled, so did the Colosseum's primary purpose. Without the spectacle of gladiators and venationes, the amphitheater lost its central role in

Roman society. The building, once a symbol of imperial power and unity, began to fade into obscurity, its grandstands empty and its roar silenced.

From Arena to Ruin: Natural Disasters and Neglect

Earthquakes and Structural Damage

The Colosseum's decline was accelerated by a series of natural disasters. Earthquakes in 442 and 508 CE caused significant structural damage, weakening the outer walls and interior arches. These seismic events marked the beginning of the amphitheater's physical collapse, leaving large sections of the structure unstable or destroyed.

One of the most devastating earthquakes struck in 1349, toppling the southern side of the Colosseum. The fallen stones were repurposed for building projects throughout Rome, including the construction of palaces, churches, and fortifications. This practice of spoliation—the reuse of materials from ancient ruins—was common in the Middle Ages, as the grandeur of Rome's past was repurposed to meet the needs of its present.

Medieval Reuse and Transformation

During the medieval period, the Colosseum took on new roles, reflecting the changing landscape of Rome. In the 6th century, it was converted into a fortress by the Frangipani family, who used its towering walls as a defensive stronghold. The arena floor and hypogeum became storage spaces, stables, and even housing for the local populace.

By the 13th century, the Colosseum was no longer a symbol of Rome's imperial might but a fragmented relic integrated into the city's evolving urban fabric. Its stones, once quarried for the amphitheater, were now a resource for new construction. Churches and palaces throughout Rome bear the marks of the Colosseum's disassembly.

Neglect and Preservation

The Renaissance brought a renewed interest in Rome's classical heritage, but the Colosseum's fortunes did not immediately improve. While artists and scholars admired its architectural brilliance, the structure itself remained vulnerable. Plants and vegetation took root in its cracks, accelerating its decay. It was not until the 18th century that systematic efforts to preserve the Colosseum began.

Pope Benedict XIV played a pivotal role in this shift. In 1749, he declared the Colosseum a sacred site, associating it with the martyrdom of early Christians—a claim not universally supported by historical evidence but influential in fostering preservation efforts. Subsequent popes and architects undertook stabilization projects, reinforcing the structure and halting its further decline.

Chapter 14:

Medieval and Renaissance Colosseum

The Colosseum, once the crown jewel of Rome's grandeur, experienced a profound transformation during the medieval and Renaissance periods. No longer echoing with the roars of crowds or the clash of gladiatorial combat, it became a silent witness to the ebb and flow of history. From serving as a quarry for construction materials to inspiring the earliest preservation efforts, the Colosseum's story during these eras reveals much about the changing priorities of a city transitioning from ancient power to modern significance.

The Colosseum as a Quarry: Reuse of Materials

A Relic Turned Resource

As the Roman Empire crumbled and the city's population dwindled, the Colosseum's utility shifted dramatically. By the early medieval period, Rome had transformed into a shadow of its former self, with its once-mighty monuments falling into disrepair. The Colosseum, no longer a center of entertainment or public life, became a vast reservoir of building materials.

The amphitheater's stones—particularly the travertine blocks that formed its outer walls—were highly prized. Durable and already cut to size, they were an invaluable resource for medieval builders who lacked the means to quarry fresh stone. Over centuries, these blocks were stripped away and repurposed for new structures. Churches, palaces, and even fortifications throughout Rome were constructed using stones from the Colosseum, embedding pieces of its history into the city's evolving skyline.

The Frangipani Fortress

During the 12th century, the Colosseum took on a new role as a fortified stronghold. The powerful Frangipani family claimed the structure and transformed it into a defensive bastion. Its massive walls and strategic location made it an ideal fortress, a symbol of power in a fragmented and feuding Rome. For a time, the Colosseum's grandeur served a practical purpose once again, albeit far removed from its original intent.

Cultural Amnesia and Pragmatism

The practice of quarrying the Colosseum persisted well into the Renaissance. Even as Rome's intellectuals began to celebrate their classical heritage, the practicality of repurposing ancient structures often outweighed the desire to preserve them. Marble from the Colosseum's interior was burned to produce lime for cement, a process that contributed to the loss of much of its decorative features. The structure's decline during this period reflects the tension between reverence for the past and the demands of a city in flux.

Early Preservation Efforts

A Sacred Transformation

The 18th century marked a turning point in the Colosseum's fortunes. Pope Benedict XIV, recognizing both its historical and spiritual significance, declared the site sacred in 1749. He associated the Colosseum with the martyrdom of early Christians, claiming that it had been a site where countless believers had been executed for their faith. While modern historians debate the accuracy of this claim, it played a crucial role in fostering a sense of reverence for the amphitheater.

To protect the Colosseum from further degradation, Benedict XIV installed Stations of the Cross within its ruins and dedicated it to the memory of Christian martyrs. This act not only halted the quarrying but also initiated a broader conversation about the importance of preserving Rome's ancient monuments.

The Birth of Preservation

The Renaissance had already seen a rekindled interest in Rome's classical past, spurred by humanists who viewed ancient art and architecture as the pinnacle of cultural achievement. By the 16th century, artists and architects such as Michelangelo and Palladio had drawn inspiration from the Colosseum, incorporating its forms into their own designs. Yet, it wasn't until the 18th and 19th centuries that systematic preservation efforts began to take shape.

Early preservationists, including archaeologists and architects, worked to stabilize the Colosseum's crumbling walls and prevent further collapse. Their efforts were driven not only by a desire to protect a piece of history but also by the recognition that the Colosseum was an invaluable cultural and artistic resource. These initiatives laid the groundwork for modern conservation practices, transforming the Colosseum from a neglected ruin into a symbol of heritage.

A Legacy of Preservation

The Colosseum's early preservation efforts reflect a broader shift in attitudes toward ancient monuments. What was once seen primarily as a resource to be exploited became a relic to be cherished. The efforts of figures like Benedict XIV and the architects of the Renaissance remind us that the preservation of history is not inevitable; it is a conscious choice, driven by a recognition of the past's value to the present and future.

Chapter 15:

Rediscovering the Colosseum: Archaeology and Restoration

For centuries, the Colosseum stood as a silent witness to the passage of time, its grand arches and battered stones weathering the rise and fall of empires. Once a symbol of Roman grandeur, it transitioned into a quarry, a fortress, and a forgotten relic. However, the rediscovery of the Colosseum in the modern era has transformed it into one of the most studied and celebrated monuments in the world. This chapter explores the journey of the Colosseum from ruin to a subject of archaeological fascination, highlighting key discoveries and the ongoing challenges of preserving this ancient wonder.

Excavations and Discoveries

Unveiling the Secrets Beneath

The 18th and 19th centuries marked the beginning of a systematic effort to uncover the secrets of the Colosseum. Driven by a renewed interest in classical antiquity during the Renaissance and Enlightenment periods, scholars and archaeologists turned their attention to Rome's most iconic structure. Early excavations focused on understanding the arena's layout and functions, particularly the enigmatic hypogeum—the underground network of tunnels and chambers that lay buried for centuries.

As archaeologists painstakingly cleared the debris, they revealed the hypogeum's intricate design. This subterranean maze, once hidden beneath the arena floor, was a marvel of Roman engineering. Featuring elevators, trapdoors, and holding areas for animals and gladiators, the hypogeum provided a glimpse into the logistical complexity behind the Colosseum's grand spectacles. The discovery of pulley systems and wooden platforms demonstrated how Roman engineers brought exotic beasts and dramatic set pieces to life, enhancing the theater of the games.

Artifacts and Inscriptions

Excavations unearthed more than just architectural wonders. Artifacts ranging from weapons and armor to pottery and coins painted a vivid picture of the Colosseum's role in Roman life. Graffiti etched into the walls revealed the thoughts and emotions of those who lived and worked within its confines. Some inscriptions recorded the names of gladiators and their victories, immortalizing these warriors in stone. Others offered a more personal touch: pleas for mercy, declarations of love, or crude humor scrawled by spectators waiting for the games to begin.

These findings humanized the Colosseum, connecting modern audiences to the individuals who lived and died in its shadow. They offered a rare glimpse into the daily lives of Romans, from the grandeur of the elite to the struggles of slaves and workers who toiled behind the scenes.

Rediscovering the Arena Floor

The arena floor itself became a focal point of archaeological study. Though much of the original wooden flooring had long since decayed, remnants of its support structures revealed how the Romans transformed the Colosseum into a dynamic stage. Sections of the floor could be removed or modified, allowing for diverse events ranging from gladiatorial combat to mock naval battles. This versatility underscored the Colosseum's role as a hub of innovation and entertainment.

Modern-Day Preservation Challenges

The Battle Against Time

Preserving the Colosseum has proven to be as daunting as uncovering its past. The structure faces relentless threats from natural forces, including rain, wind, and temperature fluctuations. These elements wear away the ancient travertine stone, weakening the arches and columns that have stood for nearly two millennia. Earthquakes, a recurring hazard in Italy, have also taken their toll, leaving cracks and instability in the monument's foundations.

Urban pollution compounds these issues. The smog and acid rain generated by Rome's bustling modern city accelerate the erosion of the Colosseum's surfaces. These environmental factors demand constant vigilance and innovative solutions from conservationists.

Managing Tourism

As one of the world's most visited landmarks, the Colosseum attracts millions of tourists annually. This influx of visitors brings both opportunities and challenges. On one hand, tourism generates revenue essential for preservation efforts. On the other, the sheer volume of foot traffic places physical stress on the structure. Steps and pathways, worn smooth by centuries of use, require regular maintenance to prevent further degradation.

To address these challenges, preservationists have implemented measures to balance accessibility with sustainability. Ticketed entry limits the number of daily visitors, while digital innovations such as virtual tours offer immersive experiences without physical strain on the monument. These strategies aim to protect the Colosseum while ensuring it remains a source of inspiration for future generations.

Cutting-Edge Restoration Techniques

Modern preservation efforts blend traditional craftsmanship with cutting-edge technology. Engineers and conservationists use laser scanning and 3D modeling to assess the Colosseum's structural integrity, creating detailed maps that guide restoration work. Damaged sections are carefully repaired with materials that match the original stone, preserving the monument's historical authenticity.

One notable restoration project involved reopening sections of the hypogeum to the public, allowing visitors to explore the underground chambers that once teemed with life. These efforts not only stabilize the Colosseum but also bring its history to life, connecting modern audiences with the ingenuity and complexity of Roman engineering.

The Ethics of Preservation

Preserving the Colosseum raises important ethical questions. Should restoration efforts aim to recreate its original splendor, or should its scars and ruins be left as a testament to the passage of time? Striking a balance between historical authenticity and modern accessibility requires thoughtful consideration. The goal is not merely to freeze the Colosseum in time but to honor its history while adapting to the needs of the present.

A Monument Reborn

The rediscovery and preservation of the Colosseum represent humanity's enduring fascination with its past. Through the efforts of archaeologists and conservationists, this ancient amphitheater has been transformed from a crumbling relic into a vibrant symbol of cultural heritage. Its excavations have deepened our understanding of Roman ingenuity, while restoration efforts ensure that its legacy endures.

Chapter 16:

A Global Symbol: The Colosseum Today

The Colosseum, with its enduring arches and timeless silhouette, has transcended its origins as an amphitheater of ancient Rome to become one of the most recognizable symbols of human history. It stands not only as a testament to Roman engineering and cultural ambition but also as a global icon that inspires awe, curiosity, and imagination. This chapter explores the Colosseum's modern role as a UNESCO World Heritage Site, its significance in tourism and popular culture, and its place in the global imagination.

The Colosseum as a UNESCO Heritage Site

Recognition and Preservation

In 1980, the Colosseum was officially designated a UNESCO World Heritage Site, cementing its status as a treasure of global cultural heritage. This recognition underscored the amphitheater's historical, architectural, and symbolic significance, while also committing resources and attention to its preservation.

The Colosseum's inclusion as a UNESCO site represents more than just its ancient roots. It is a symbol of resilience, having survived earthquakes, wars, and centuries of neglect. Its story mirrors the broader narrative of humanity's ability to endure and adapt. UNESCO's designation highlights the Colosseum's role as a universal reminder of our shared history, bridging cultures and eras.

Preservation Efforts and Global Collaboration

As a UNESCO site, the Colosseum benefits from international funding and expertise aimed at preserving its integrity for future generations. Restoration projects have included cleaning its travertine façade, reinforcing its foundations, and stabilizing its walls. Advanced technologies, such as 3D scanning and structural monitoring, have been employed to better understand the amphitheater's condition and predict potential risks.

Preservation is not without challenges. Pollution from Rome's bustling urban environment accelerates the wear on its ancient stones, while the constant flow of tourists adds additional strain. Despite these challenges, ongoing efforts reflect a commitment to safeguarding the Colosseum as a global symbol of history and culture.

Tourism, Film, and the Modern Imagination

A Magnet for Global Visitors

Each year, millions of tourists flock to the Colosseum, making it one of the most visited landmarks in the world. For many, stepping into the Colosseum is akin to stepping back in time. Visitors are transported to an era of gladiators and emperors, their imaginations ignited by the sheer scale and grandeur of the structure.

Guided tours and exhibitions delve into the amphitheater's history, offering insights into its construction, the spectacles it hosted, and the lives of those who passed through its gates. Interactive experiences, including virtual reality reconstructions, allow visitors to visualize the Colosseum in its prime, complete with roaring crowds and dramatic performances.

The Colosseum's status as a tourist destination has also spurred economic activity, supporting local businesses and providing jobs. However, managing this influx of visitors requires careful planning to balance accessibility with preservation. Measures such as timed entry, restricted access to certain areas, and digital alternatives aim to protect the monument while enhancing the visitor experience.

The Colosseum in Film and Media

The Colosseum's iconic status extends far beyond its physical presence. It has become a fixture in film, literature, and art, often serving as a symbol of both the grandeur and the decline of ancient Rome. From the epic sets of *Ben-Hur* (1959) to the digitally reconstructed arena in *Gladiator* (2000), the Colosseum has captivated audiences around the world, bringing its history to life on the big screen.

These portrayals, though sometimes romanticized or historically inaccurate, have played a crucial role in cementing the Colosseum's place in the modern imagination. They evoke the drama and spectacle of the Roman Empire while inviting contemporary audiences to reflect on themes of power, ambition, and mortality.

Beyond film, the Colosseum appears in countless other media, from video games like *Assassin's Creed* to novels and documentaries. These representations ensure that the Colosseum remains a relevant and compelling subject, inspiring new generations to explore its history.

A Symbol of Resilience and Hope

In modern times, the Colosseum has taken on new meanings. It has become a backdrop for global events and a platform for raising awareness about social and humanitarian issues. The amphitheater is often illuminated in different colors to mark occasions such as World Heritage Day or to draw attention to causes like the abolition of the death penalty.

As a symbol of resilience, the Colosseum reminds us of humanity's ability to endure and adapt. Its battered walls and enduring arches are a testament to the passage of time and the power of preservation, reflecting both the fragility and the strength of human achievement.

THE COLOSSEUM IN CONTEXT

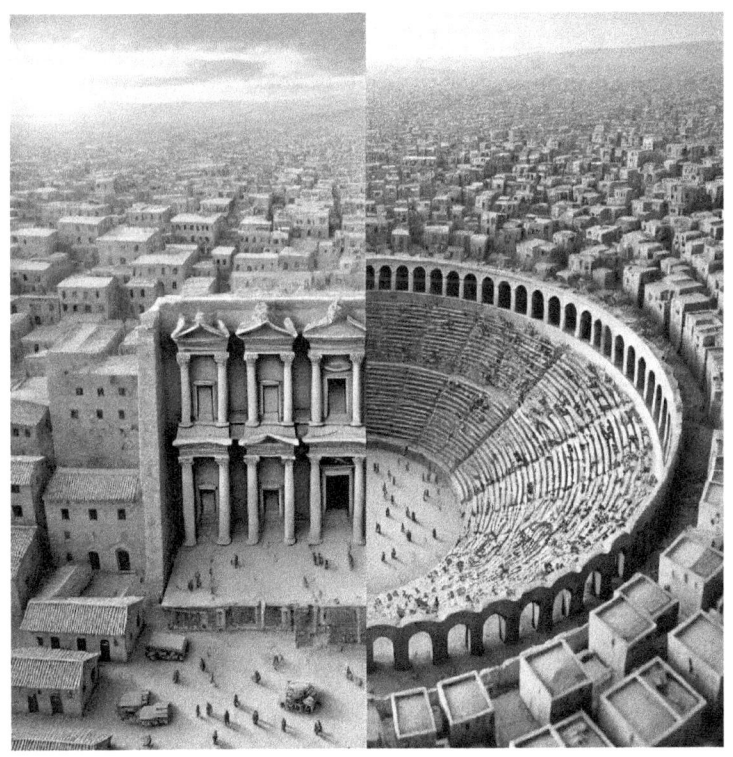

Chapter 17:

Comparisons with Other Roman Amphitheaters

The Colosseum is undoubtedly the crown jewel of Roman amphitheaters, but it is far from the only one. Across the Roman Empire, amphitheaters rose as symbols of power, culture, and communal entertainment. These structures, while often overshadowed by the Colosseum, reveal the breadth of Roman architectural ingenuity and the diversity of experiences they offered to their communities. This chapter explores the amphitheaters scattered across the empire, comparing their design, purpose, and legacy to that of the Colosseum, and examining what makes Rome's iconic structure truly stand apart.

Amphitheaters Across the Empire

A Network of Entertainment

By the height of the Roman Empire, more than 230 amphitheaters dotted its vast territories, ranging from the

Italian Peninsula to the remote provinces of North Africa, Gaul, and Britain. These structures were built to host a variety of spectacles, including gladiatorial games, venationes (wild animal hunts), and public executions. While they varied in size and design, they shared a common purpose: to reinforce Roman culture and values while providing entertainment.

Verona Arena

One of the best-preserved Roman amphitheaters, the Verona Arena in northern Italy, stands as a testament to Roman engineering. Built in the 1st century CE, around the same time as the Colosseum, it could hold approximately 30,000 spectators. Unlike the Colosseum, which was partially dismantled over centuries, the Verona Arena has retained much of its structure and continues to host events today, including concerts and opera performances. Its longevity as a functional venue highlights the adaptability of Roman design.

El Djem Amphitheater

In modern-day Tunisia, the El Djem Amphitheater stands as one of the most impressive examples outside Italy. Built in the 3rd century CE, it could accommodate up to 35,000 spectators, rivaling the Colosseum in size. El Djem's remote location underscores the reach of Roman architectural ambition, bringing monumental structures to even the fringes of the empire. Its design mirrors the Colosseum's elliptical shape and multi-tiered seating, though it lacks the same level of intricate decoration and subterranean complexity.

The Amphitheater of Pompeii

The Amphitheater of Pompeii, built in 70 BCE, is one of the oldest surviving Roman amphitheaters. Its simple design reflects the architectural experimentation of the Republic era. With a capacity of around 20,000, it served as a hub for gladiatorial games and other events in the thriving city. Unlike the Colosseum, it lacks the sophisticated hypogeum and grand façade, but its preservation under volcanic ash provides invaluable insights into early Roman amphitheater construction.

Roman Britain's Amphitheaters

In the far reaches of the empire, amphitheaters in Roman Britain, such as those in Chester and Caerleon, demonstrate how the Romans adapted their architecture to local conditions. These amphitheaters were smaller and often built with local materials, but they served the same purpose: to entertain and Romanize the local population. They reflect how the concept of the amphitheater was not limited to Rome but was a portable symbol of imperial culture.

How the Colosseum Stands Apart

Unmatched Scale and Innovation

The Colosseum's size alone sets it apart from its counterparts. With a seating capacity of over 50,000, it dwarfs most other Roman amphitheaters. Its elaborate design, featuring four stories of travertine stone and a complex network of arches, showcases a level of ambition unparalleled in the ancient world. The hypogeum, with its elevators and trapdoors, added a level of dynamism and spectacle that other amphitheaters could not replicate.

The Colosseum also incorporated state-of-the-art engineering. The use of concrete—a Roman innovation—allowed for larger, more durable structures. Its system of vomitoria (exit passages) enabled rapid crowd dispersal, a feature that inspired the design of modern stadiums.

A Centerpiece of Propaganda

While other amphitheaters served local populations, the Colosseum was a symbol of imperial power and generosity. Commissioned by Emperor Vespasian and completed by his sons Titus and Domitian, it was a gift to the people of Rome and a statement of the Flavian dynasty's legitimacy. The inaugural games, which lasted 100 days and featured unprecedented spectacles, set the tone for the Colosseum's role as a stage for imperial propaganda.

The Colosseum's location in the heart of Rome further emphasized its importance. Built on the site of Nero's infamous Domus Aurea, it represented a reclamation of space for public use, reinforcing the idea that the emperor served the people. This political and symbolic significance elevated the Colosseum above other amphitheaters, making it a centerpiece of Roman identity.

Artistic and Cultural Impact

The Colosseum's intricate decorations, including marble statues, frescoes, and reliefs, reflected the artistic sophistication of Rome at its peak. Though much of this ornamentation has been lost, historical accounts and archaeological findings suggest that the Colosseum was as much a cultural showcase as a venue for bloodsport.

Its influence extended beyond its own time. While other amphitheaters were functional, the Colosseum became a symbol of Rome itself. In the centuries following its decline, it inspired countless works of art, literature, and architecture, cementing its place in the global imagination.

Legacy and Preservation

Unlike many other Roman amphitheaters, the Colosseum has been the subject of extensive preservation efforts, ensuring its survival as a cultural icon. While structures like the Verona Arena and El Djem Amphitheater are celebrated for their state of preservation, the Colosseum's ongoing restoration projects highlight its unique status as a global heritage site. Its designation as a UNESCO World Heritage Site and its continued role as a tourist destination and cultural symbol underscore its enduring legacy.

Chapter 18:

The Colosseum's Influence on Architecture

The Colosseum, with its grand arches and ingenious design, is not merely a relic of ancient Rome; it is a cornerstone of architectural innovation. Its influence has rippled across centuries, shaping the principles of design and construction in ways that continue to resonate today. From the advancements in Roman engineering that revolutionized building techniques to its enduring legacy in the design of modern sports stadiums, the Colosseum stands as a testament to humanity's ability to blend functionality with grandeur. This chapter explores the architectural innovations introduced by the Colosseum and their profound impact on the world.

Roman Innovations that Shaped the World

Mastering Arches and Vaults

One of the most striking features of the Colosseum is its use of arches and vaulted spaces. The Romans perfected the arch, transforming it from a simple structural element into a hallmark of monumental architecture. The Colosseum's design incorporates hundreds of arches, which not only enhance its aesthetic appeal but also provide remarkable strength and stability. These arches distribute weight evenly, allowing the structure to support massive loads while maintaining a sense of openness and lightness.

The use of barrel and groin vaults within the Colosseum further showcased Roman ingenuity. These vaults created expansive, unobstructed spaces, enabling the construction of the hypogeum, corridors, and vomitoria (exit passages). This mastery of vaulted design became a cornerstone of Roman architecture, influencing everything from aqueducts to basilicas.

Revolutionizing Construction Materials

The Colosseum is a masterpiece of material innovation. Roman engineers pioneered the use of concrete, a versatile and durable material that revolutionized construction. Unlike earlier civilizations that relied on labor-intensive stone blocks, the Romans used a mix of lime, volcanic ash, and aggregate to create concrete. This allowed for faster construction and greater flexibility in design.

Travertine, a type of limestone, was used for the Colosseum's façade and main structural elements, while brick-faced concrete formed the core of the walls and vaults. The combination of materials ensured both strength and cost-efficiency. This approach to construction not only made the Colosseum possible but also laid the groundwork for future architectural marvels.

Crowd Management and Urban Planning

The Colosseum's design reflects a deep understanding of crowd management and urban planning. Its system of vomitoria allowed for the efficient movement of over 50,000 spectators, enabling the arena to be filled or emptied in minutes. This innovation was crucial for maintaining order and ensuring the safety of attendees.

The amphitheater's placement within Rome's urban fabric was equally strategic. Built on the site of Nero's Domus Aurea, it symbolized a return of public space to the people. Its location near the Forum and other key landmarks reinforced its role as a centerpiece of civic life, influencing how cities were designed to integrate monumental structures with everyday urban activity.

The Arena's Legacy in Modern Sports Stadiums

A Template for Spectator Comfort

Modern sports stadiums owe much to the Colosseum's pioneering design. Its tiered seating arrangement, which provided clear sightlines for spectators at every level, remains a foundational principle in stadium architecture. The amphitheater's elliptical shape ensured that all seats were oriented toward the action, a feature that modern venues strive to replicate.

The Colosseum's velarium, a retractable awning that shaded spectators from the sun, was an early example of environmental control in architecture. Operated by skilled sailors, this system demonstrated the Romans' ability to enhance spectator comfort—a goal that continues to drive innovations in modern stadium design, from retractable roofs to climate-controlled interiors.

Efficiency and Accessibility

The Colosseum's efficient layout and accessibility set a benchmark for stadium design. Its network of entrances and exits allowed for seamless crowd flow, minimizing congestion and ensuring safety. This principle has been adopted in contemporary venues, where wide concourses, multiple entry points, and accessible seating are standard features.

Additionally, the Colosseum's use of designated seating areas based on social hierarchy prefigured modern stadium zoning, where different ticket tiers determine access to specific sections. While modern stadiums aim for inclusivity, the underlying principle of organizing large crowds into manageable segments remains the same.

Inspiration for Iconic Venues

The Colosseum's influence can be seen in some of the world's most famous stadiums. London's Wembley Stadium, New York's Madison Square Garden, and Melbourne's MCG all incorporate design elements that echo the Roman amphitheater. Even contemporary architectural marvels, such as the Allianz Arena in Munich and the Beijing National Stadium (Bird's Nest), draw inspiration from the Colosseum's balance of form and function.

These modern arenas, like the Colosseum, are more than venues for entertainment; they are symbols of civic pride and technological advancement. By blending cutting-edge engineering with a focus on spectator experience, they continue the legacy of Rome's architectural ingenuity.

A Timeless Blueprint

The Colosseum's influence on architecture is a testament to the enduring power of Roman innovation. Its mastery of materials, structural design, and spatial organization set a standard that has shaped human creativity for millennia. From the grand amphitheaters of the Roman Empire to the state-of-the-art stadiums of today, the Colosseum remains a timeless blueprint for architects and engineers.

Chapter 19:

Myths, Legends, and Misconceptions

The Colosseum's enduring presence has made it fertile ground for myths, legends, and misconceptions that have shaped its story over the centuries. From tales of Christian martyrs to dramatic but exaggerated depictions of its spectacles, the amphitheater's history is intertwined with narratives that often blur the lines between fact and fiction. This chapter explores the most persistent myths and misconceptions, uncovering the truths behind these stories and examining why they continue to captivate the imagination.

The Truth About Christian Martyrs in the Arena

A Long-Standing Myth

One of the most pervasive myths about the Colosseum is its association with the mass martyrdom of Christians. For centuries, the amphitheater has been depicted as a site where countless Christians were thrown to lions or executed for their faith. Paintings, novels, and films have immortalized this narrative, embedding it in popular culture and religious memory.

However, historical evidence for these events is surprisingly sparse. While it is true that Christians were persecuted during certain periods of the Roman Empire, including the infamous reigns of Nero and Diocletian, there is no definitive proof that the Colosseum served as a primary venue for their executions. Most recorded martyrdoms occurred in other locations, such as the Circus of Nero, near the Vatican.

The association likely gained traction during the Middle Ages and Renaissance when the Colosseum was reinterpreted as a sacred site. Pope Benedict XIV reinforced this connection in 1749 by consecrating the Colosseum as a memorial to Christian martyrs, despite the lack of corroborating historical evidence. The monument's dramatic setting and its history of violent spectacles made it an evocative symbol, even if the reality was more nuanced.

Christian Symbolism and the Colosseum

While the myth of mass martyrdom may not align with historical facts, the Colosseum's symbolic association with Christianity remains powerful. The structure is often used as a backdrop for events commemorating religious freedom and human rights. Its consecration as a place of memory reflects its transformation from a site of spectacle and bloodshed to one of reflection and reverence.

Stories That Captivate the Imagination

The Gladiators' Last Stand

Another enduring legend involves the gladiators who fought in the Colosseum. Popular depictions often portray them as noble warriors who fought for their freedom against impossible odds. While some gladiators did earn their liberty through victory, the reality of their lives was far more complex. Most were slaves, prisoners of war, or criminals forced into combat. Their status as entertainment assets meant they were often well-trained and cared for—but always expendable.

The romanticized image of gladiators as rebels or champions for justice, seen in films like *Gladiator* (2000), owes more to modern storytelling than historical records. While stories of defiant gladiators, such as the rebellion led by Spartacus, capture the imagination, they were exceptions rather than the rule. For most, the arena was not a path to glory but a brutal and often short-lived existence.

Exotic Animals and Wild Beasts

The Colosseum's venationes, or wild animal hunts, have inspired countless tales of exotic creatures and daring encounters. Lions, tigers, elephants, and even crocodiles were indeed brought to the arena from across the Roman Empire, showcasing Rome's dominion over nature. However, some stories stretch the bounds of credibility. Accounts of entire naval battles staged in the flooded arena or massive herds of animals unleashed at once often exaggerate the logistical and practical realities of such events.

Still, the inclusion of these creatures in the games was an extraordinary feat of logistics and spectacle. Their presence symbolized Rome's vast reach and ability to command the natural world, even if some of the more extravagant tales are better suited to myth than history.

The Colosseum and the "Thumbs Down" Gesture

One of the most iconic images associated with the Colosseum is the "thumbs down" gesture, supposedly used by Roman emperors to signal the death of a defeated gladiator. This trope has been immortalized in art and cinema, creating a dramatic moment where life and death hang on a single gesture.

However, historical accounts suggest that the reality was more nuanced. The precise gestures used in the arena remain a topic of debate among scholars. Roman texts describe gestures such as the "pollice verso" (turned thumb), but their exact meaning is unclear. Some interpretations suggest that a thumb pointed upward or horizontally might have indicated death, while a closed fist or hidden thumb signaled mercy. The "thumbs down" we associate with condemnation is likely a modern reinterpretation, shaped more by 19th-century art than ancient Roman practice.

The Power of Myth and Misconception

Why Myths Persist

The myths and legends surrounding the Colosseum endure because they fulfill a human need for drama, heroism, and moral lessons. The amphitheater's history is rich with spectacle and violence, providing fertile ground for imaginative storytelling. Whether it is the defiant gladiator, the persecuted martyr, or the exotic beast, these stories resonate because they reflect timeless themes of struggle, survival, and identity.

Cultural Reinterpretation

Over the centuries, the Colosseum has been reinterpreted to suit the values and narratives of different eras. In medieval and Renaissance Europe, it became a symbol of Christian sacrifice and redemption. In the modern age, it represents the ingenuity and ambition of ancient Rome. These shifting interpretations highlight the Colosseum's versatility as a cultural icon, capable of embodying different meanings for different audiences.

Chapter 20:

The Colosseum as a Metaphor

The Colosseum is more than an ancient amphitheater; it is a symbol that transcends its physical structure. Its enduring presence evokes themes of power, spectacle, and decline, offering a lens through which we can examine the trajectory of civilizations and the human condition. This chapter delves into how the Colosseum serves as a metaphor, exploring the lessons it offers about history, culture, and the resilience of humanity.

Power, Spectacle, and Decline: Lessons from History

The Apex of Roman Power

The Colosseum stands as a monument to the zenith of Roman power. Commissioned by Emperor Vespasian and completed under Titus and Domitian, it was a bold statement of the empire's wealth, engineering prowess, and control over vast resources. Constructed using advanced techniques and materials sourced from across the empire, the Colosseum symbolized Rome's ability to conquer not only lands but also the constraints of nature and time.

Its very existence reflected the might of the Flavian dynasty, which sought to legitimize its rule by gifting this monumental structure to the people of Rome. The games held within its walls, featuring exotic animals, gladiators, and elaborate set pieces, were designed to awe the masses and reinforce the emperor's divine authority. The Colosseum became a stage where power was performed and celebrated, a reminder of Rome's unparalleled dominance.

The Role of Spectacle in Society

The Colosseum also highlights the role of spectacle as a tool for social cohesion and control. The phrase "bread and circuses" encapsulates the Roman strategy of placating the masses with free food and grand entertainment. The games served to distract citizens from the harsh realities of their lives, providing a sense of unity and shared identity through collective participation in the spectacle.

Yet, the Colosseum's emphasis on spectacle also underscores the dangers of excess and the ethical compromises made in the pursuit of entertainment. The bloodshed and brutality that defined its games raise questions about the cost of spectacle and the ways societies justify cruelty in the name of cultural or political aims. These themes resonate in modern contexts, where mass entertainment often reflects societal values and tensions.

The Inevitability of Decline

The Colosseum's eventual decline mirrors the trajectory of Rome itself. As the empire's power waned, so too did the amphitheater's prominence. Natural disasters, economic challenges, and shifting cultural values led to its disrepair and repurposing. From a symbol of imperial might, it became a quarry, a fortress, and eventually a ruin—a stark reminder of the impermanence of even the greatest achievements.

This cycle of rise and fall is a recurring theme in history. The Colosseum's decay invites us to reflect on the fragility of civilizations and the forces that contribute to their decline. It reminds us that no empire is immune to the passage of time and the inevitability of change.

What the Colosseum Teaches Us About Civilization

The Balance Between Progress and Humanity

The Colosseum encapsulates the tension between technological progress and ethical considerations. Its construction was a feat of engineering brilliance, showcasing the ingenuity of Roman architects and builders. However, its purpose—to host violent spectacles for mass consumption—raises questions about the societal values that drove such innovation.

This duality invites us to consider the ways in which modern societies balance progress with humanity. The Colosseum's history challenges us to reflect on how we use technology and resources, asking whether our advancements serve the common good or perpetuate cycles of exploitation and inequality.

The Importance of Cultural Memory

The Colosseum's survival through centuries of neglect and repurposing underscores the importance of cultural memory. It has been a quarry, a fortress, a site of Christian veneration, and a global tourist destination, each iteration adding layers to its story. Today, it stands not only as a relic of the past but as a symbol of resilience and continuity.

By preserving monuments like the Colosseum, we maintain a connection to our shared history, ensuring that the lessons of the past are not forgotten. The Colosseum teaches us that cultural heritage is not static; it evolves, gaining new meanings and relevance with each generation.

A Reflection of Humanity's Contradictions

The Colosseum is, above all, a reflection of humanity's contradictions. It embodies both the heights of artistic and architectural achievement and the depths of human cruelty. It represents the capacity for both creation and destruction, beauty and brutality.

This duality makes the Colosseum a powerful metaphor for civilization itself. It reminds us that progress is often accompanied by compromise, and that the legacies we leave behind are shaped as much by our triumphs as by our failings.

CONCLUSION

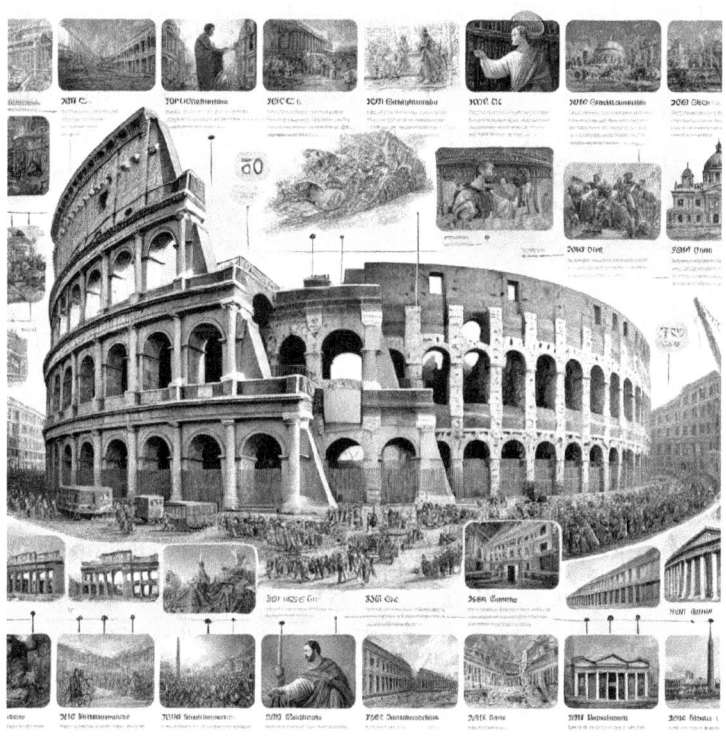

The Colosseum's Timeless Appeal

The Colosseum's enduring allure lies in its ability to transcend time and context, captivating the imaginations of people across centuries and continents. As an architectural masterpiece, it inspires awe with its monumental scale, ingenious design, and intricate engineering. As a cultural artifact, it serves as a bridge between ancient and modern worlds, offering insights into the complexities of Roman civilization and its values.

What makes the Colosseum truly timeless is its dual identity as both a relic of antiquity and a living monument. Its weathered stones and open arches tell a story of resilience and transformation. Once a stage for gladiators and emperors, it now hosts millions of visitors each year, each of them drawn by a desire to connect with the grandeur and legacy of ancient Rome. The Colosseum's ability to remain relevant in an ever-changing world underscores its significance as a symbol of human achievement and aspiration.

Reflections on the Rise and Fall of Rome

The Colosseum is not merely a symbol of Roman grandeur; it is also a reflection of the empire's trajectory—from its rise to its eventual decline. Built at the height of Roman power, it epitomized the empire's ability to mobilize vast resources, innovate with groundbreaking techniques, and create structures that embodied its identity and ambition. It was a place where emperors displayed their authority, the populace reveled in spectacle, and the might of Rome was on full display.

Yet, the Colosseum also reminds us of the fragility of even the greatest civilizations. As Rome's power waned, so too did the Colosseum's prominence. Natural disasters, economic challenges, and cultural shifts led to its neglect and repurposing. Its stones were quarried, its corridors abandoned, and its grandeur faded into ruin. This cycle of rise and fall mirrors the impermanence of empires, serving as a cautionary tale about the forces that shape history.

Rome's decline was not sudden; it was a gradual unraveling influenced by internal strife, external pressures, and shifting priorities. The Colosseum, as a microcosm of the empire, illustrates how cultural and political hubris can give way to decay, and how the passage of time reshapes even the most enduring legacies.

Lessons from History: Power, Innovation, and Legacy

The Colosseum offers profound lessons about power, innovation, and legacy. Its construction was a testament to the extraordinary capabilities of Roman engineering and the ambition of its leaders. The use of arches, concrete, and advanced crowd-management systems revolutionized architecture and influenced the design of public spaces for millennia. These innovations highlight the potential of human ingenuity to create structures that are both functional and beautiful.

However, the Colosseum also serves as a reminder of the ethical dilemmas that often accompany progress. The spectacles it hosted, though awe-inspiring, were marked by violence and exploitation. Gladiatorial combat, animal hunts, and public executions reveal the darker side of Roman society, where entertainment often came at the cost of human and animal suffering. This duality invites reflection on how societies balance progress with humanity, and how the pursuit of power and spectacle can obscure the values that sustain civilizations.

Finally, the Colosseum's legacy underscores the importance of preservation and cultural memory. Its survival through centuries of neglect and repurposing is a testament to the efforts of those who recognized its significance and worked to protect it. Today, it stands as a symbol of resilience and continuity, reminding us that the stories we choose to preserve shape how we understand our past and envision our future.

A Monument to Humanity

The Colosseum is more than a structure; it is a narrative etched in stone. It tells the story of a civilization at its zenith, the complexities of its values, and the enduring impact of its innovations. It is a place where history, culture, and imagination converge, offering lessons that are as relevant today as they were two thousand years ago.

APPENDICES

Timeline of the Colosseum's History

Pre-Colosseum Era

- **64 CE**: The Great Fire of Rome devastates much of the city. Emperor Nero seizes the opportunity to construct his lavish Domus Aurea (Golden House) on the cleared land, including an artificial lake.
- **69 CE**: The Year of the Four Emperors sees political chaos and the rise of the Flavian dynasty under Vespasian.

Construction and Inauguration

- **70 CE**: Emperor Vespasian begins construction of the Flavian Amphitheater (later known as the Colosseum) on the site of Nero's artificial lake, reclaiming the land for public use.
- **80 CE**: The Colosseum is completed under Emperor Titus and inaugurated with 100 days of games, featuring gladiatorial combat, animal hunts, and mock naval battles.

- **81-96 CE**: Emperor Domitian adds the hypogeum (underground network) and other enhancements to the Colosseum.

Peak Use

- **1st-2nd Century CE**: The Colosseum hosts regular games and spectacles, including gladiatorial contests, venationes (animal hunts), and public executions.
- **2nd Century CE**: Notable emperors like Trajan and Hadrian use the Colosseum to reinforce their power and generosity through grand spectacles.

Decline of Spectacles

- **4th Century CE**: Gladiatorial games begin to wane due to changing societal values and the rise of Christianity.
- **325 CE**: Emperor Constantine bans the use of criminals for gladiatorial combat, signaling a decline in the games.
- **404 CE**: Emperor Honorius officially ends gladiatorial combat following the martyrdom of Saint Telemachus.

Transformation and Neglect

- **6th Century CE**: The Colosseum is repurposed as housing, a fortress, and later a quarry for building materials.
- **1349 CE**: A massive earthquake collapses parts of the southern wall, marking a turning point in the Colosseum's decline.

Rediscovery and Preservation

- **1749 CE**: Pope Benedict XIV consecrates the Colosseum as a sacred site dedicated to Christian martyrs, halting its quarrying.
- **19th Century CE**: Archaeological excavations begin, revealing the hypogeum and other features.
- **1980 CE**: The Colosseum is designated a UNESCO World Heritage Site.
- **21st Century CE**: Modern restoration projects continue, preserving the Colosseum as a global icon and major tourist destination.

Glossary of Terms and Key Figures

Terms

- **Amphitheater**: An open-air venue with tiered seating, used for public spectacles such as gladiatorial combat, animal hunts, and executions.
- **Hypogeum**: The underground complex beneath the Colosseum's arena, featuring tunnels, chambers, and mechanisms for staging events.
- **Velarium**: A retractable awning used to provide shade for spectators in the Colosseum.
- **Venationes**: Spectacles involving the hunting or combat of wild animals in the arena.
- **Vomitoria**: Passageways in the Colosseum's seating area designed to enable efficient crowd movement.
- **Pollice verso**: A debated Roman gesture, often interpreted as the "thumbs up" or "thumbs down" used to signal a gladiator's fate.

Key Figures

- **Vespasian (69-79 CE)**: The emperor who initiated the construction of the Colosseum, reclaiming land for public use and establishing the Flavian Amphitheater as a gift to the Roman people.

- **Titus (79-81 CE)**: Vespasian's son and successor, who completed the Colosseum and inaugurated it with a grand series of games.
- **Domitian (81-96 CE)**: The youngest son of Vespasian, who added the hypogeum and other architectural enhancements to the Colosseum.
- **Constantine the Great (272-337 CE)**: The first Christian emperor of Rome, who enacted reforms that curtailed gladiatorial games and shifted the empire's values.
- **Honorius (384-423 CE)**: The emperor who officially banned gladiatorial combat, marking the end of an era for the Colosseum.
- **Pope Benedict XIV (1675-1758)**: The pontiff who consecrated the Colosseum as a sacred site, initiating its transformation into a monument of Christian memory.

www.ingramcontent.com/pod-product-compliance
Lightning Source LLC
Chambersburg PA
CBHW071551220526
45469CB00003B/983